READY, SET, GO!

New York State

Grade 4
Mathematics Test

Staff of Research & Education Association

Research & Education Association
Visit our website at
www.rea.com

The Learning Standards presented in this book were created and implemented by the New York State Education Department (NYSED). For further information, visit the NYSED website at *www.emsc.nysed.gov/3-8/e-home.htm.*

Research & Education Association
61 Ethel Road West
Piscataway, New Jersey 08854
E-mail: info@rea.com

Ready, Set, Go!
New York State
Grade 4 Mathematics Test

Printed in the United States of America

Library of Congress Control Number 2009934097

ISBN-13: 978-0-7386-0713-9
ISBN-10: 0-7386-0713-4

REA® is a registered trademark of Research & Education Association, Inc.

Contents

About Research & Education Association

Founded in 1959, Research & Education Association (REA) is dedicated to publishing the finest and most effective educational materials—including software, study guides, and test preps—for students in elementary school, middle school, high school, college, graduate school, and beyond.

Today REA's wide-ranging catalog is a leading resource for teachers, students, and professionals.

We invite you to visit us at *www.rea.com* to find out how "REA is making the world smarter."

Acknowledgments

We would like to thank Larry B. Kling, Vice President, Editorial, for his overall guidance, which brought this publication to completion; Pam Weston, Vice President, Publishing, for setting the quality standards for production integrity and managing the publication to completion; Diane Goldschmidt, Senior Editor, for editorial project management; Alice Leonard, Senior Editor, for preflight editorial review; and Christine Saul, Senior Graphic Designer, for designing our cover.

We also gratefully acknowledge the numerous educators, writers, and editors for their guidance and work, and BBE Associates, Ltd., for content development, project management, typesetting, and final review.

Introduction

Welcome to an Educational Adventure

The New York State Testing Program is the Empire State's answer to the federal No Child Left Behind Act, which requires that states use standards-based testing to ensure that students are picking up the skills and knowledge necessary for academic success.

We at REA believe that a friendly, hands-on introduction and preparation for the test are keys to creating a successful testing experience. REA's NY State Testing Program books offer these key features:

✓ Clearly identified book activities

✓ Contextual illustrations

✓ Easy-to-follow lessons

✓ Step-by-step examples

✓ Tips for solving problems tailored for the proper grade level

✓ Exercises to sharpen skills

✓ Lots of practice

Below is helpful information for students, parents, and teachers concerning the NY State Test and test taking in general. Organized practice is itself a prime skill for young students to master, because it will help set the tone for success long into the future as their educational adventure continues. It is REA's sincere hope that this book—by providing relevant, standards-based practice—can become an integral part of that adventure.

What is the New York State Test?

The New York State Test is a standards-based assessment used in New York's public schools. Performance on the New York State Test equates not with the grades students receive for teacher-assigned work but rather with proficiency measures pegged to how well students are acquiring the knowledge and skills outlined in the New York State Learning Standards. Those proficiency measures fall into three broad categories, or bands: "partially proficient," "proficient," and "advanced proficient."

When is the NY State Mathematics Test given?

The test is administered in early spring. Grade 4 students take the NY State Mathematics Test on three consecutive days. Each day requires 50 minutes, plus an additional 10 minutes of preparation time.

What is the format of the NY State Mathematics Test?

On Day 1, students answer 30 multiple-choice questions. For each multiple-choice question, students are asked to choose the correct answer out of four. On Day 2, students answer 7 short-response questions and 2 extended-response questions. On Day 3, students answer 7 short-response questions and 2 extended-response questions. For these open-ended questions, students answer with written responses in their own words.

Understanding the NY State Mathematics Test and This Book

Students:

This book was specially written and designed to make test practice easy and fruitful for students. Our practice tests are very much like the actual NY State Mathematics Test, and our review is filled with illustrations, drills, exercises, and practice questions to help students become familiar with the testing environment and to retain information about key topics.

Parents:

The NY State Mathematics Test and other state assessment tests are designed to give the school information about how well children are achieving in the areas required by the New York State Learning Standards. These standards describe what students should know at the end of certain grades. This book helps children review and prepare effectively and positively for the NY State Mathematics Test.

Teachers:

Teachers introduce students to the test-taking environment and the demands of the NY State Mathematics Test. Teachers can use our authoritative book in the classroom for planned, guided instruction and practice testing. Effective preparation means better test scores!

Information about the New York State Testing Program

For more information about the New York State Testing Program, contact the New York State Department of Education:

www.emsc.nysed.gov

General Information
Telephone: 518-474-3852

Mailing address:
New York State Education Department
89 Washington Avenue
Albany, NY 12234

Test Accommodations and Special Situations

Every effort is made to provide a level playing field for students with disabilities who are taking the NY State Mathematics Test. In general, students with educational disabilities should be provided with the testing accommodations specified in their Individualized Education Programs (IEPs) or Section 504 Accommodation Plans (504 Plans) when taking the test. However, testing accommodations that change the measurement of a skill being tested are not permitted on the NY State Mathematics Test.

Testing accommodations in students' IEPs or 504 Plans that are reading-related—for example, reading the test to the student—are permitted for the NY State Mathematics Test. However, test questions must never be changed or simplified, nor may the school provide additional examples.

Because the NY State Mathematics Test assesses students' ability to calculate, the use of a calculator or mathematical tables are not allowed for Grade 4. Students whose IEPs or 504 Plans specify the use of an abacus will be allowed to use such an item with this test.

Tips for Test Taking

- **Do your homework.** From the first assignment of the year, organize the day so there is always time to study and keep up with homework.

- **Communicate.** If there are any questions, doubts, or concerns about anything relating to school, study, or tests, speak up. This goes for teachers and parents, as well as students.

- **Get some rest.** Getting a good night's sleep the night before the test is essential to waking up sharp and focused.

- **Eat right.** Having a good breakfast—nothing very heavy—the morning of the test is what the body and mind need. Comfortable clothes, plenty of time to get to school, and the confidence of having prepared properly are all any student needs.

- **Test smart.** Read the questions carefully. Make sure answers are written correctly in the proper place on the answer sheet. Don't rush, and don't go too slow. If there is time, go back and check questions that you weren't sure about.

Format and Scoring of the NY State Mathematics Test

The questions on the NY State Mathematics Test can contain items and concepts learned in earlier grades. For fourth graders, the mathematics test takes place over three consecutive days. The test takes about 50 minutes of testing time per day, not including time for distributing and collecting materials and reading directions. The school provides a ruler for each student.

The NY State Grade 4 Mathematics Test contains a total of 48 test items. Thirty of the items are multiple-choice. The test also contains fourteen short-reponse questions and four extended-response questions.

Each multiple-choice question is worth 1 point. The most a student can score on the multiple-choice questions is 30 points. Short-response questions are worth 2 points each, and extended-response questions are worth 3 points each. The most a student can score on the 18 open-ended questions combined is 40 points. The highest score a student can receive on the NY State Grade 4 Mathematics Test is 70 points.

Each day's testing session is timed. If students have not finished a section when time runs out, they must stop and put down their pencils. There are clear directions throughout the test.

Core Curriculum Content Strands in Mathematics

The NY State Mathematics Test is not diagnostic, but is designed to measure how well students are achieving the New York State Learning Standards. The NY State Learning Standards determine what students should know and be able to do at certain grade levels. The NY State Mathematics Test assesses five Core Curriculum Content Strands in mathematics. The distribution of these strands in the test is as follows:

- 47.1% (33) of the points on the NY 4 Math Test assess Number Sense and Operations

- 15.7% (11) of the points on the NY 4 Math Test assess Algebra

- 12.9% (9) of the points on the NY 4 Math Test assess Geometry

- 14.3% (10) of the points on the NY 4 Math Test assess Measurement

- 10% (7) of the points on the NY 4 Math Test assess Statistics and Probability

Each standard of the CCCS has Cumulative Progress Indicators (CPIs). (See the following table.) All strands are tested on the NY State Mathematics Test, but not all CPIs are. The CPIs that coordinate with each strand are included here.

CCCS Mathematics Standards on the NY 4 State Math Test

Strand	CCCS Band	CPI	Chapter in This Book
Number Sense and Operations	Number Systems	4.N.1-12	Chapter 1: Number Sense
	Number Theory	4.N.13	Chapter 2: Operations
	Operations	4.N.14-25	Chapter 2: Operations
	Estimation	4.N.26-27	Chapter 3: Estimation
Algebra	Variables and Expressions	4.A.1	Chapter 6: Algebra
	Equations and Inequalities	4.A.2-3	Chapter 6: Algebra
	Patterns, Relations, and Functions	4.A.4-5	Chapter 6: Algebra
Geometry	Shapes	4.G.1-5	Chapter 4: Geometry
	Geometric Relationships	4.G.6-8	Chapter 4: Geometry
Measurement	Units of Measurement	4.M.1-7	Chapter 5: Measurement
	Units	4.M.8-10	Chapter 5: Measurement

Statistics and Probability	Collection of Data	4.S.1-2	Chapter 7: Statistics and Probability
	Organization and Display of Data	4.S.3	Chapter 7: Statistics and Probability
	Analysis of Data	4.S.4	Chapter 7: Statistics and Probability
	Predictions from Data	4.S.5-6	Chapter 7: Statistics and Probability

Chapter 1

Number Sense

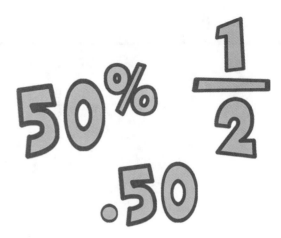

Numbers are everywhere. You see numbers when you look in the telephone book. You use numbers to tell time. Your height and weight are given in numbers. Each number represents a value. For example, the number 10,000 is less than the number 100,000. This chapter will help you to understand the value of very small numbers and numbers greater than one million. It will also show you how to compare numbers and put them in a certain order, such as from least to greatest.

To understand numbers, you should also know the **value** of decimals and fractions. You need to know, for example, that 0.50 is equal to $\frac{1}{2}$. In this chapter, you will also learn about those concepts.

Whole Numbers

A **whole number** is an integer. An **integer** is a number on a number line. Zero is a whole number. Positive numbers are whole numbers. The numbers 1, 2, 3, 4, and 5 are positive numbers. Negative numbers are also integers. The numbers $-1, -2, -3, -4,$ and -5 are negative numbers. The digits in whole numbers have a value, called a **place value**. The diagram that follows shows the place values for the number 100,000—one hundred thousand.

```
  ↑    ↑    ↑    ↑    ↑    ↑
hundred thousand
     ten thousand
          thousand
               hundred
                    ten
                         one

  1    0   0,   0    0    0
```

Notice the use of commas to help you determine the value of a large number. The commas divide the number, from right to left, into groups of three. The three numbers in each group have ones, tens, and hundreds places, but the second group from the right is thousands, so they are thousands, ten thousands, and hundred thousands. Look at this number:

3,285

In this number, the 3 is in the one thousands place, the 2 is in the hundreds place, the 8 is in the tens place, and the 5 is in the ones place. So you would read it as "three thousand two hundred eighty-five."

Now look at this number:

32,850

In this number, the 3 is in the ten thousands place, the 2 is in the one thousands place, the 8 is in the hundreds place, the 5 is in the tens place, and the 0 is in the ones place. So you would read it as "thirty-two thousand eight hundred fifty."

Now let's look at a much larger number. The next group of three to the left of thousands is millions, and it follows the same pattern.

3,285,000

In this number, the 3 is in the millions place, the 2 is in the hundred thousands place, the 8 is in the ten thousands place, and the 5 is in the thousands place. There are zeros in the hundreds, tens, and ones places. You would read this number as "three million two hundred eighty-five thousand."

Look at the chart below. Notice that each time a zero is added to the end of the number, the number moves up in place value and gets larger.

1   one

10   ten

100   one hundred

1,000   one thousand

10,000   ten thousand

100,000   one hundred thousand

1,000,000   one million

As you've seen, numbers can be represented as words. Look at the following:

Eight thousand seven hundred twenty-nine

This is the same as the number 8,729. Now try this exercise for practice.

Circle the number that is the same as six thousand three hundred twelve.

3,612   6,012   6,312   612

The correct answer is 6,312.

Comparing Numbers by Place Value

Knowing place value helps you compare numbers. Try this exercise for practice.

Which of the following numbers is largest? Circle it.

5,882   5,873   5,894

All three have the same digits in the thousands place and the hundreds place. Move to the tens place. 5,894 has the largest digit in the tens place: 9. It must be larger than the other two numbers.

Practice Questions

Practice 1: Whole Numbers and Place Value

DIRECTIONS:

Choose the best of the answer choices given for each of the following problems. Fill in the circle next to your choice.

1. Each year, about 350,000 people visit the Baseball Hall of Fame in Cooperstown, New York. What is the value of the 5 in the number 350,000?

   Ⓐ 5 hundreds

   Ⓑ 5 thousands

   Ⓒ 5 ten thousands

   Ⓓ 5 hundred thousands

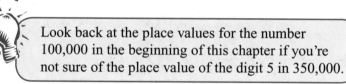

Look back at the place values for the number 100,000 in the beginning of this chapter if you're not sure of the place value of the digit 5 in 350,000.

2. The population of New York City is about 8,274,527. What is the value of the 4 in the number 8,274,527?

   Ⓐ 4 thousands

   Ⓑ 4 ten thousands

   Ⓒ 4 hundred thousands

   Ⓓ 4 millions

What is the place value of the 1 in the number 1,000 on page 3?

3. During the year, four thousand eight hundred forty-four books were checked out of the Medford town library. What is another way to write this number?

    Ⓐ 484

    Ⓑ 4,844

    Ⓒ 4,804

    Ⓓ 4,484

HINT

If you're unsure about the answer, say the number quietly to yourself. Ask yourself what number is in the thousands place, the hundreds place, the tens place, and the ones place.

4. Which of the following numbers is largest?

    Ⓐ 12,128

    Ⓑ 12,348

    Ⓒ 12,448

    Ⓓ 12,438

HINT

If you're having trouble with the answer, go back and look at the diagram of the number 100,000 on page 2. Think about how you can compare the numbers in the different columns.

Fractions

You just learned about whole numbers. A fraction is not a whole number. It is part of a number. A fraction tells how many parts of something you have. The *total* number of parts goes on the bottom. This is the **denominator**. The number of parts *you* have goes on the top. This is the **numerator**. An easy way to remember this is to remember that the **d**enominator goes **d**own at the bottom of the fraction.

Suppose your family ordered a pizza with six slices.

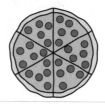

The pizza has six slices, so six is the denominator. In this case, the denominator tells how many slices of pizza make up the whole pizza. Now imagine that you eat one slice of pizza. This means that you eat one part of the pizza. The fraction showing how much of the pizza you eat is $\frac{1}{6}$.

Circle the numerator in each of the fractions below.

$$\frac{1}{2} \qquad \frac{1}{3} \qquad \frac{8}{13} \qquad \frac{5}{16}$$

If you circled the 1, 1, 8, and 5, you are correct. If you missed any, review what a numerator is in the discussion on fractions.

Fractions appear on the number line between whole numbers. Look at this number line:

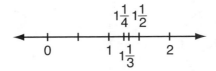

Notice that $1\frac{1}{2}$ is between 1 and 2, and $1\frac{1}{3}$ is also between 1 and 2.

Which Is Greater?

If you want to know which of two fractions is greater, and the denominators are the same, this is easy to do. The fraction with the larger numerator is greater. For example, $\frac{5}{7}$ is greater than $\frac{4}{7}$.

If the denominators are different, however, it is harder to tell which fraction is larger. If two fractions have the same numerators but different denominators, the fraction with the smaller denominator is the larger of the two. For example, $\frac{3}{4}$ is greater than $\frac{3}{5}$.

If you have a diagram with the fractional parts shaded, you can usually see which fraction is larger.

As an example, look at the **shaded** circles below.

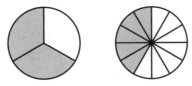

By looking at the circles, you can see that $\frac{2}{3}$ is definitely greater than $\frac{5}{12}$.

Look at the fractions below. On the line below the fractions, write them in order from GREATEST to LEAST. Use the shaded diagrams to help you.

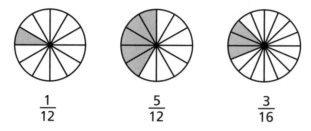

$$\frac{1}{12} \qquad \frac{5}{12} \qquad \frac{3}{16}$$

If you wrote $\frac{5}{12}$, $\frac{3}{16}$, $\frac{1}{12}$, you are right. Look carefully at the shaded parts of the circles if you didn't get this right.

Equivalent Fractions

Some fractions stand for the same amount, even though they have different numerators and denominators. These are called **equivalent fractions**. Look at these fractions.

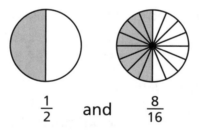

$$\frac{1}{2} \quad \text{and} \quad \frac{8}{16}$$

From the shaded parts of the circles, you can see that the fractions $\frac{1}{2}$ and $\frac{8}{16}$ have the same value, even though they are written in different ways.

Compare the fractions below. Write < (less than), > (greater than), or = for each pair of fractions. Use the shaded circles to help you choose the right answer.

1. $\frac{1}{6}$ ☐ $\frac{4}{7}$

2. $\frac{4}{5}$ ☐ $\frac{7}{8}$

3. $\frac{3}{5}$ ☐ $\frac{3}{4}$

4. $\frac{2}{9}$ ☐ $\frac{4}{12}$

You are correct if your answers are

1. $\frac{1}{6} < \frac{4}{7}$

2. $\frac{4}{5} < \frac{7}{8}$

3. $\frac{3}{5} < \frac{3}{4}$

4. $\frac{2}{9} < \frac{4}{12}$

If you missed one or more, review the section on fractions.

Practice Questions

Practice 2: Fractions

DIRECTIONS:

Choose the best of the answer choices given for each of the following problems. Fill in the circle next to your choice.

1. Compare the shaded regions. Which symbol belongs in the box?

$$\frac{5}{12} \;\square\; \frac{3}{16}$$

Ⓐ <

Ⓑ >

Ⓒ =

Ⓓ None of the above

Look carefully at the shaded areas. Which is bigger?

2. Which list shows the fractions in order from least to greatest?

Ⓐ $\frac{1}{3}, \frac{1}{2}, \frac{1}{4}$

Ⓑ $\frac{1}{3}, \frac{1}{4}, \frac{1}{2}$

Ⓒ $\frac{1}{2}, \frac{1}{3}, \frac{1}{4}$

Ⓓ $\frac{1}{4}, \frac{1}{3}, \frac{1}{2}$

HINT

Think about how to compare fractions. If the numerators are all the same, compare denominators; the fraction with the largest denominator is smallest in value.

3. Of the squares Shania drew, $\frac{3}{9}$ are shaded.

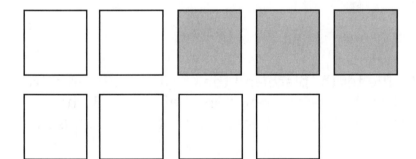

Which fraction is equivalent to $\frac{3}{9}$?

Ⓐ $\frac{1}{3}$

Ⓑ $\frac{1}{4}$

Ⓒ $\frac{2}{3}$

Ⓓ $\frac{1}{2}$

HINT

Remember: equivalent fractions stand for the same amount.

Decimals

Like whole numbers, decimals have **place values**. Look at the diagram below for 0.62.

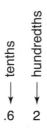

Notice that the place value for decimals is similar to that of whole numbers—but the place value moves to the right, and the place value gets *smaller* rather than larger, so that "hundredths" is larger than "thousandths." Notice that "th" is added to the end of each value for decimals, and there is no place value for "one-ths."

Look at this decimal:

.34

In this decimal, the 3 is in the tenths place and the 4 is in the hundredths place. If you add a zero after the decimal point and before the 3, the number is .034, which is smaller than .34, because 0 tenths (in .034) is smaller than 3 tenths (in .34).

A mixed decimal has a whole number and a decimal. A mixed decimal is always greater than a decimal. Look at these numbers:

1.25 > 0.25

But what if two numbers are both mixed decimals? If they have different whole number parts, the one with the greater whole number is greater. If they have the same whole number part, the one with the greater decimal is greater. For example,

3.27 > 2.74

1.25 > 1.15

You can also write equivalent forms of fractions as decimals. Look at the following pairs.

$$0.25 = \frac{1}{4}$$

$$0.5 = \frac{1}{2}$$

$$0.75 = \frac{3}{4}$$

$$2.25 = 2\frac{1}{4}$$

Decimals and Money

Decimals are used to write money values. Numbers to the left of the decimal point represent dollars. Numbers to the right of the decimal point represent cents. Seven dollars and 52 cents is written as a decimal like this:

$$\$7.52$$

Notice that the $ sign shows that the number stands for an amount of money.

Here are the major coins and bills expressed as decimals.

5 dollars = $5.00

1 dollar = $1.00

1 quarter = $0.25

1 dime = $0.10

1 nickel = $0.05

1 penny = $0.01

Practice Questions

Practice 3: Decimals and Money

DIRECTIONS:

Choose the best of the answer choices given for each of the following problems. Fill in the circle next to your choice.

1. **Which group of numbers is in order from least to greatest?**

   Ⓐ .34   1.24   1.0

   Ⓑ .34   1.0   1.24

   Ⓒ 1.24   1.0   .34

   Ⓓ 1.0   .34   1.24

HINT

> Remember that a whole number is greater than a decimal, and if you have two mixed decimals with the same whole number part, choose the one with the greater decimal.

2. **Which group of numbers is in order from least to greatest?**

   Ⓐ 1.50   .99   1.23

   Ⓑ .99   1.50   1.23

   Ⓒ 1.23   1.50   .99

   Ⓓ .99   1.23   1.50

HINT

> The number with only the decimal is the smallest.

3. **Which decimal is equivalent to $3\frac{3}{4}$?**

    Ⓐ 1.75

    Ⓑ 3.25

    Ⓒ 3.3

    Ⓓ 3.75

HINT

If you have trouble with this question, look at the list of decimals and equivalent fractions on page 13. What is 0.75 as a fraction?

4. **Hannah has 8 dollars and 77 cents. Which of the following shows this amount in decimal form?**

    Ⓐ $8.77

    Ⓑ $8.07

    Ⓒ $87.70

    Ⓓ $0.87

HINT

Remember that in money notation, dollars are whole numbers and cents are decimals.

Practice Questions

End-of-Chapter Practice Problems

DIRECTIONS:

Choose the best of the answer choices given for each of the following problems. Fill in the circle next to your choice.

1. Which group of numbers is in order from least to greatest?

    Ⓐ 2.0   .90   2.09

    Ⓑ .90   2.0   2.09

    Ⓒ 2.09   .90   2.0

    Ⓓ 2.0   2.09   .90

     HINT

    In a decimal, .0 is less than .09.

2. Compare the shaded regions. Which symbol belongs in the box?

    $\frac{5}{9}$ □ $\frac{3}{8}$

    Ⓐ <

    Ⓑ >

    Ⓒ =

    Ⓓ None of the above

     HINT

    Compare the shaded portions of the two circles.

3. The lottery prize in the state of New York is worth 9,125,000 dollars. What is the value of 1 in the number 9,125,000?

    Ⓐ 1 thousand

    Ⓑ 1 ten thousand

    Ⓒ 1 hundred thousand

    Ⓓ 1 million

> If you can't figure out the value of 1, go back and look at the place values in the number 1,000,000 found toward the beginning of the chapter.

4. Which decimal is equivalent to $2\frac{1}{4}$?

    Ⓐ 1.25

    Ⓑ 2.25

    Ⓒ 2.45

    Ⓓ 2.50

> If you have trouble with this question, look at the list of decimals and equivalent fractions on page 13. What is the decimal value for one-fourth?

5. Which of the following fractions is smallest?

    Ⓐ $\frac{1}{5}$

    Ⓑ $\frac{1}{3}$

    Ⓒ $\frac{1}{2}$

    Ⓓ $\frac{1}{4}$

> Notice that all the numerators are the same in these fractions. In this case, you should compare denominators.

6. About 6,234,000 schoolchildren wear eyeglasses. What is the value of 4 in the number 6,234,000?

    Ⓐ   4 hundreds

    Ⓑ   4 thousands

    Ⓒ   4 ten thousands

    Ⓓ   4 hundred thousands

HINT

The 4 is in the second grouping of three numbers.

7. Jamaal spent 6 dollars and 32 cents at the movies on Saturday. Which of the following shows this amount in decimal form?

    Ⓐ $3.32

    Ⓑ $3.62

    Ⓒ $6.02

    Ⓓ $6.32

HINT

Remember that dollars are whole numbers and cents are decimals.

8. Sang-mi has the beads shown below. What fraction of them are blue?

    Ⓐ $\frac{1}{2}$

    Ⓑ $\frac{1}{3}$

    Ⓒ $\frac{1}{4}$

    Ⓓ $\frac{1}{6}$

HINT

Use what you know about equivalent fractions to find the correct answer.

Chapter 2

Operations

In Chapter 1, you learned that a number's place value determines how large or small it is. You learned that fractions and decimals stand for parts of numbers. You compared numbers in different forms and put them in order from least to greatest.

In this chapter, you'll practice solving problems for which you have to add, subtract, multiply, and divide numbers. This is called using mathematical **operations**. You'll notice that some of these problems are easier to answer than others. Usually, you can answer the easier questions by using **mental math**. When you use mental math, you figure out the answer in your head. For other questions, you'll have to use pencil and paper to figure out the answer.

You will also add and subtract money amounts in dollars and cents.

Adding and Subtracting Whole Numbers

You can usually use mental math to solve easier problems. For example, look at the problem on the next page:

Find the exact answer: 2,000 + 5,000

    Ⓐ   3,000

    Ⓑ   6,000

    Ⓒ   7,000

    Ⓓ   8,000

You should be able to answer this question quickly by using mental math. You know that 2 + 5 = 7, so 2,000 + 5,000 = 7,000. Answer choice C is the correct answer.

Let's try another.

Find the exact answer: 45,732 − 44,732

    Ⓐ   100

    Ⓑ   1,000

    Ⓒ   1,500

    Ⓓ   10,000

This question can also be solved easily by using mental math. You should see that the numbers are the same except for the digits in the thousands place. The first number has 1 more thousand than the second number. Answer choice B is correct.

Not all problems can be solved this quickly, however. Try to solve the following problem.

Find the exact answer: 582 + 145

   Ⓐ 349

   Ⓑ 437

   Ⓒ 727

   Ⓓ 737

You probably can't solve this problem in your head. If you are not allowed to use a calculator, you'll need to use a pencil and paper. Set up the problem like this:

$$\begin{array}{r} 582 \\ +\ 145 \\ \hline \end{array}$$

When you set up the problem this way, it's easy to add the numbers. You can tell that the correct answer choice is C, 727.

Let's try another.

Find the exact answer: 7,034 − 2,569

   Ⓐ 3,475

   Ⓑ 3,495

   Ⓒ 4,375

   Ⓓ 4,465

You need a pencil and paper to answer this problem, too. If you use a pencil and paper, set up the problem this way:

$$\begin{array}{r} 7,034 \\ -2,569 \\ \hline \end{array}$$

If you set up the problem this way, you can easily subtract the numbers and get 4,465 (answer choice D).

Now let's try a **word problem**.

Karen has sold 210 tickets to raise money for her school. Her family bought 120 of these tickets. How many tickets did Karen sell to people other than her family?

Ⓐ 80

Ⓑ 90

Ⓒ 110

Ⓓ 120

To find out how many tickets Karen sold to people other than her family, you need to subtract 120 from 210. If you use a pencil and paper to solve this problem, set it up like this:

$$\begin{array}{r} 210 \\ -\ 120 \\ \hline \end{array}$$

When you subtract these numbers, you'll see that Karen sold 90 tickets to people other than her family. Answer choice B is correct.

Practice Questions

Practice 4: Adding and Subtracting Whole Numbers

DIRECTIONS:

Choose the best of the answer choices given for each of the following problems. Fill in the circle next to your choice. You may NOT use a calculator.

1. **Find the exact answer: 324 + 548**

    Ⓐ 762

    Ⓑ 772

    Ⓒ 862

    Ⓓ 872

HINT
Use a pencil and paper to line up the numbers. Then add the numbers.

2. **Find the exact answer: 8,295 − 340**

    Ⓐ 7,842

    Ⓑ 7,855

    Ⓒ 7,955

    Ⓓ 8,025

HINT
Use a pencil and paper to line up the numbers so that 8,295 is on the top and 340 is on the bottom. Then subtract the numbers.

3. **Find the exact answer: 2,131 + 679**

   Ⓐ 2,810

   Ⓑ 2,808

   Ⓒ 2,710

   Ⓓ 2,709

HINT

Set up the problem correctly and then add the numbers.

4. **Michelle has a comic book collection. She had 125 comic books, and her grandmother gave her 98 more. How many comic books does she have in all?**

   Ⓐ 122

   Ⓑ 123

   Ⓒ 222

   Ⓓ 223

HINT

You need to add the two numbers to get the right answer.

Directions for the Open-Ended Question

The following question is an open-ended question. Remember to:

Read the question carefully and think about the answer.

Answer all the parts of the question.

Show your work or explain your answer.

5. **William has a stamp collection. He had 210 stamps, and his sister gave him 30 more. Then William gave 53 stamps to his friend. How many stamps does William have now?**

    Show your work.

    Answer: _____ **stamps**

HINT

You have to show how you got your answer to this problem. It involves both addition and subtraction.

Operations with Fractions and Decimals

Before you add or subtract fractions, make sure the denominators are the same. Then add or subtract the numerators.

$$\frac{3}{5} + \frac{1}{5} = \frac{4}{5}$$

$$\frac{8}{16} - \frac{5}{16} = \frac{3}{16}$$

To add and subtract two or more decimals, make sure the decimal points are aligned. Then perform the operation. Look at the following chart. It shows the places for whole numbers, tenths, and hundredths.

	Whole	Tenths	Hundredths
	2	5	7
PLUS	1	2	2
EQUALS	3	7	9

This addition problem can also be set up like this:

$$\begin{array}{r} 2.57 \\ +\,1.22 \\ \hline 3.79 \end{array}$$

The same thing can be done when subtracting decimals.

	Whole	Tenths	Hundredths
	4	6	2
MINUS	3	4	1
EQUALS	1	2	1

$$\begin{array}{r} 4.62 \\ -\,3.41 \\ \hline 1.21 \end{array}$$

You can also use decimal notation to add or subtract amounts of money. What is the sum for the addition problem below?

$$\begin{array}{r} \$2.30 \\ \$0.62 \\ +\$1.35 \\ \hline \end{array}$$

Did you say $4.27? If so, you are correct! This is four dollars and twenty-seven cents. Always remember to place the dollar sign beside your answer when dealing with amounts of money.

Practice Questions

Practice 5: Operations with Fractions and Decimals

DIRECTIONS:

Choose the best of the answer choices given for each of the following problems. Fill in the circle next to your choice. You may NOT use a calculator.

1. **Find the exact answer:** $\frac{5}{12} - \frac{1}{12}$

   Ⓐ $\frac{4}{5}$

   Ⓑ $\frac{4}{12}$

   Ⓒ $\frac{1}{12}$

   Ⓓ $\frac{4}{7}$

HINT

Check to see if the denominators are the same. If they are, then subtract the second numerator from the first numerator.

2. **What is the result when you subtract 0.45 from 4.45?**

Ⓐ 4

Ⓑ 0.4

Ⓒ 0.04

Ⓓ 0.004

Use mental math to get the answer. Notice that both 0.45 and 4.45 have "45" to the right of the decimal point. What is left after you subtract?

Directions for the Open-Ended Question

The following question is an open-ended question. Remember to:

Read the question carefully and think about the answer.

Answer all the parts of the question.

Show your work or explain your answer.

3. **Archie has $3.00 to spend at the school festival. He buys a snow cone for $0.50 and a barbecue sandwich for $1.25. How much money does Archie have left?**

Show your work.

Answer: _____

First, add together the two items that Archie bought. Then subtract that total from the original amount he brought to the festival.

Multiplying and Dividing Numbers

On the NY State Mathematics Test, you may have to multiply or divide numbers using pencil and paper.

Find the exact answer: 848 ÷ 4

- Ⓐ 212
- Ⓑ 222
- Ⓒ 301
- Ⓓ 312

Set up the problem using pencil and paper like this:

$$4\overline{)848}$$

Did you get 212? You are correct.

Let's try another one:

Find the exact answer: 42 × 15

- Ⓐ 210
- Ⓑ 620
- Ⓒ 630
- Ⓓ 740

To solve this problem by using a pencil and paper, set it up like this:

$$\begin{array}{r} 42 \\ \times\ 15 \\ \hline \end{array}$$

The correct answer is 630.

Let's try one more:

Mrs. Harris bought juice boxes in packs of 6 for her students. Which of these could be the total number of juice boxes that she bought without having any left over?

- Ⓐ 22
- Ⓑ 24
- Ⓒ 28
- Ⓓ 32

To answer this question, you have to choose the answer choice into which 6 can be divided evenly. If you divide 6 into 22, you get 3.6666, so this is not the correct answer. If you divide 6 into 24, you get 4. The number 6 does not divide evenly into 28 and 32, so answer choice B, 24, is the only correct answer.

A related idea in division is the **remainder**. If you divide 6 into 26, you get a quotient of 4 with a remainder of 2. In other words,

$$26 = 6 \times 4 + 2$$

The remainder is what is left over when a number does not divide evenly into another number.

Practice Questions

Practice 6: Multiplying and Dividing Numbers

DIRECTIONS:

Choose the best of the answer choices given for each of the following problems. Fill in the circle next to your choice. You may NOT use a calculator.

1. **Find the exact answer: 360 ÷ 2**

   Ⓐ 130

   Ⓑ 170

   Ⓒ 180

   Ⓓ 190

HINT

You might be able to solve this problem by using mental math. If not, set up the problem like this:
$2\overline{)360}$

2. **Find the exact answer: 38 × 24**

   Ⓐ 228

   Ⓑ 812

   Ⓒ 822

   Ⓓ 912

HINT

Set up the problem like this: $\begin{array}{r} 38 \\ \times\ 24 \end{array}$

Directions for the Open-Ended Question

The following question is an open-ended question. Remember to:

Read the question carefully and think about the answer.

Answer all the parts of the question.

Show your work or explain your answer.

3.   Jeremy has 172 stickers to give to 8 friends. He wants to give an equal number of stickers to each friend. How many stickers will he give to each friend? How many stickers will he have left, if any?

Show your work.

Number of stickers for each friend: _____

Number of stickers left over: _____

HINT

Divide 172 by 8. Is there a remainder?

Multiplication Rules

The following are some rules that will help you answer questions involving multiplication.

- You can multiply numbers in any order and get the same answer. This is called the **commutative property** of multiplication.

  For example, $7 \times 3 = 21$ is the same as $3 \times 7 = 21$.

- You can also multiply numbers in any order when you are multiplying more than two numbers. The idea that you can multiply three or more numbers in any order is called the **associative property** of multiplication. Multiply the numbers in parentheses first.

  For example, $(7 \times 3) \times 2 = 42$ is the same as $7 \times (3 \times 2) = 42$.

- Any number multiplied by 1 is that number. The number 1 is called the **identity element** of multiplication.

  For example, $8 \times 1 = 8$, and $105 \times 1 = 105$.

- Any number multiplied by 0 is 0.

  For example, $9 \times 0 = 0$, and $72 \times 0 = 0$.

Practice Questions

Practice 7: Multiplication Rules

DIRECTIONS:

Choose the best of the answer choices given for each of the following problems. Fill in the circle next to your choice.

1. If $45 \times \square = 0$, what is the value of $\square$?

   Ⓐ 0

   Ⓑ 1

   Ⓒ 5

   Ⓓ 45

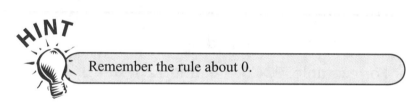

Remember the rule about 0.

2. Which of the following is the same as $2 \times (60 \times 4)$?

   Ⓐ $2 + (60 \times 4)$

   Ⓑ $4 \div (2 \times 60)$

   Ⓒ $(2 \times 60) \times 4$

   Ⓓ $2 \times 2 \times (60 \times 4)$

Go back and reread the rule about the associative property of multiplication if you don't know the answer to this question.

3. If 100 × ☐ = 100, then what is the value of ☐?

 Ⓐ 0

 Ⓑ 1

 Ⓒ $\frac{1}{2}$

 Ⓓ 100

Remember that the number 1 is the identity element for multiplication.

4. According to the commutative property of multiplication, **7 × 3** is the same as

 Ⓐ 3 × 0

 Ⓑ (7 × 1) + 3

 Ⓒ 3 × 7

 Ⓓ 7 × 1

Go back and reread the rule about the commutative property of multiplication if you don't know the answer to this question.

Practice Questions

End-of-Chapter Practice Problems

DIRECTIONS:

Choose the best of the answer choices given for each of the following problems. Fill in the circle next to your choice. You may NOT use a calculator.

1. **Find the exact number: 2,517 + 3,893**

    Ⓐ 5,990

    Ⓑ 6,410

    Ⓒ 6,420

    Ⓓ 7,510

These number are too large to add with mental math. Stack them and add them together.

2. **Mr. Renfro bought markers in packs of 12 for his art students. Which of these could be the total number of markers that he bought without having any markers left over?**

    Ⓐ 14

    Ⓑ 26

    Ⓒ 36

    Ⓓ 40

You will be able to divide 12 exactly into the correct answer choice.

3. **Find the exact answer: 2,420 ÷ 2**

    Ⓐ 1,210

    Ⓑ 1,200

    Ⓒ 1,190

    Ⓓ 1,010

You can use mental math here. Divide 2 into 2,000. Then divide 2 into 400. Then divide 2 into 20.

4. **Rosalinda has collected 148 different soda pop bottles. She gave 73 of the bottles to the American History Museum. How many bottles does she have left?**

    Ⓐ 65

    Ⓑ 73

    Ⓒ 74

    Ⓓ 75

Subtract 73 from 148 to see how many bottles Rosalinda has left.

5. **Find the exact answer: 67 × 19**

    Ⓐ 670

    Ⓑ 770

    Ⓒ 1,273

    Ⓓ 1,274

Stack the numbers so that you can multiply them more easily.

6. **Find the exact answer: 3.74 + 1.63**

   Ⓐ 5.27

   Ⓑ 5.37

   Ⓒ 5.87

   Ⓓ 6.37

> Remember to keep the decimal points in line as you write the problem.

7. **A farmer sells apples for $0.35 each. Martina buys 4 apples and gives the farmer $2.00. How much change will she receive?**

   Ⓐ $0.35

   Ⓑ $0.60

   Ⓒ $0.65

   Ⓓ $1.40

> Begin by multiplying $0.35 by 4. Then subtract this amount from $2.00.

8. **What does *n* equal in 172 × *n* = 0?**

   Ⓐ 0

   Ⓑ 1

   Ⓒ −1

   Ⓓ −172

> Remember the multiplication rule about zero.

Directions for the Open-Ended Question

The following question is an open-ended question. Remember to:

Read the question carefully and think about the answer.

Answer all the parts of the question.

Show your work or explain your answer.

9. **Mrs. Akiro has 98 beads to make 8 bracelets. She wants to put an equal number of beads on each bracelet. How many beads will she put on each bracelet? How many beads will be left over?**

   Show your work.

   Number of beads for each bracelet: _____

   Number of beads left over: _____

Divide 98 by 8. What is the remainder?

Chapter 3

Estimation

How long do you think it will take you to finish reading this chapter? You don't know for sure, since you just started. But you could probably **estimate**—or guess—how long it would take. Do you think it might take an hour? That's a good estimate.

For questions that ask you to estimate, you can usually figure out a **range of values** that includes the exact answer. Many of the questions in Chapter 2 asked you to find the exact answer, but sometimes all that is needed is an answer choice that is close to the exact answer, as you will learn in this chapter. You will NOT be allowed to use a calculator for estimation questions on the NY State test.

Rounding

You can use mental math to answer some estimation questions. Remember that when you use mental math, you figure out the answer in your head without using a pencil and paper or a calculator.

For most questions, the best way to estimate is to **round** numbers. You can round numbers to the nearest 10 or the nearest 100, for example. When you round to the nearest 10, you look closely at the number in the ones place. If the number in the ones place is 5 or more, you round up, and if the number is 4 or less, you round down.

The numbers below are rounded to the nearest 10.

Number	Rounded to Nearest 10
23	20
34	30
67	70
78	80
91	90

For the number 23, 3 is in the ones place. The number 3 is less than 4, so you round down to 20 rather than up to 30. So the number 23 rounded to the nearest 10 is 20. See how it works?

Round each of these numbers to the nearest 10.

Number	Rounded to Nearest 10
11	_____
15	_____
24	_____
37	_____
42	_____
59	_____
65	_____

You are correct if your answers are:

Number	Rounded to Nearest 10
11	10
15	20
24	20
37	40
42	40
59	60
65	70

If you missed any of these answers, go back to check the digit in the ones place. Remember that a 5 gets rounded up, not down.

When you round to the nearest 100, you look closely at the number in the tens place and ignore the number in the ones place. Just as with rounding to the nearest 10, if the number in the tens place is 5 or greater, you round up, and if this number is 4 or less, you round down. These numbers are rounded to the nearest 100:

Number	Rounded to Nearest 100
123	100
182	200
214	200
356	400
479	500
591	600

Now you try it.

Round each of these numbers to the nearest 100.

Number	Rounded to Nearest 100
115	_____
179	_____
234	_____
390	_____
450	_____
625	_____

You are correct if your answers are:

Number	Rounded to Nearest 100
115	100
179	200
234	200
390	400
450	500
625	600

If you missed any of these, go back to check the number in the tens place. Remember that if the number in the tens place is 5, the number gets rounded up, not down. Also, the numbers in the ones place are not used when rounding to the nearest 100.

Estimating Addition

When you estimate addition problems, the answer options usually give you a **range**. A range has two numbers, and the exact answer is somewhere between these two numbers. For addition, you estimate the **sum**, which is the number you get when you add two numbers together. Look at the problem below:

Estimate 813 + 279. The sum is between which numbers?

Ⓐ   50 and 400

Ⓑ   450 and 700

Ⓒ   750 and 1,000

Ⓓ   1,050 and 1,300

To answer this problem, you need to round 813 to the nearest 100. So 813 is rounded to 800. Then round 279 to the nearest 100. That's 300. Now add these numbers together. You get 1,100. The number 1,100 is between 1,050 and 1,300, so answer choice D is correct.

Let's try another one.

When Charlene added 319 and 897, she got the sum of 1,216. Use estimation to see if that sum is reasonable.

Round 319 to the nearest hundred. It's 300. Now round 897 to the nearest hundred. It's 900. Add these two numbers together: 300 + 900 = 1,200. This is very close to 1,216, so Charlene's answer is reasonable.

Practice Questions

Practice 8: Estimating Addition

DIRECTIONS:

Choose the best of the answer choices given for each of the following problems. Fill in the circle next to your choice. You may **NOT** use a calculator.

1. **Estimate 680 + 292. The sum is between which numbers?**

    Ⓐ 400 and 600

    Ⓑ 700 and 800

    Ⓒ 900 and 1,100

    Ⓓ 1,300 and 1,500

 Round 680 and 292 to the nearest 100. Then add those two numbers together.

2. **Estimate 109 + 258. The sum is between which numbers?**

    Ⓐ 100 and 200

    Ⓑ 300 and 600

    Ⓒ 600 and 800

    Ⓓ 800 and 1,000

 Round 109 and 258 to the nearest 100. Then add those two numbers together.

Estimating Subtraction

Questions that ask you to estimate subtraction are set up just like questions that ask you to estimate addition. They ask you to choose the correct range of numbers. For subtraction, however, you'll look for the **difference** instead of the sum. Let's try this one:

Estimate 678 − 214. The difference is between which numbers?

 Ⓐ 50 and 400

 Ⓑ 450 and 700

 Ⓒ 750 and 1,000

 Ⓓ 1,050 and 1,300

To answer this question, round 678 to 700 and 214 to 200. Then subtract 200 from 700. The answer is 500, so answer choice B is correct.

Let's try another problem.

When Robert subtracted 522 from 895, he got 273 for the answer. Use estimation to see if Robert's answer is reasonable.

Round 895 to the nearest hundred. It's 900. Now round 522 to the nearest hundred. It's 500. Subtract: 900 − 500 = 400. This is not very close to 273, so Robert's answer is not reasonable. Sure enough, Robert has made an error in subtracting. The actual answer is 373, which is much closer to the estimate of 400. This shows why it is important to use estimation to see if an answer is reasonable.

Practice Questions

Practice 9: Estimating Subtraction

DIRECTIONS:

Choose the best of the answer choices given for each of the following problems. Fill in the circle next to your choice. You may NOT use a calculator.

1. **Estimate 780 − 349. The difference is between which numbers?**

   Ⓐ   100 and 299

   Ⓑ   300 and 399

   Ⓒ   400 and 599

   Ⓓ   600 and 899

> Round 780 and 349 to the nearest 100. Then subtract the smaller number from the larger number and choose the correct answer choice.

2. **Estimate 836 − 432. The difference is between which numbers?**

   Ⓐ   1,200 and 1,500

   Ⓑ   1,000 and 1,100

   Ⓒ   700 and 900

   Ⓓ   200 and 500

> Begin by rounding both numbers to the nearest 100. Then subtract the second number from the first, and choose the right range.

Estimating Multiplication

For multiplication problems, you estimate the **product**, which is the number you get when you multiply two numbers together. Rounding will help you to estimate the product. Look at this problem:

Estimate 38 × 22. The product is between which numbers?

    Ⓐ 30 and 70

    Ⓑ 80 and 150

    Ⓒ 300 and 700

    Ⓓ 800 and 1,500

To estimate the answer to this problem, round 38 to the nearest 10, which is 40. Round 22 to the nearest 10, which is 20. When you multiply 40 × 20, the answer is 800. Answer choice D is the correct answer.

Let's try one more.

When Syreeta multiplied 48 × 29, she got a product of 1,392. Use estimation to see if Syreeta's answer is reasonble.

To estimate the answer to this problem, round 48 to the nearest 10, which is 50. Then round 29 to the nearest 10, which is 30. Multiply these numbers. Your estimated answer is 1,500. This is close to Syreeta's product of 1,392. Her answer is reasonable.

Practice Questions

Practice 10: Estimating Multiplication

DIRECTIONS:

Choose the best of the answer choices given for each of the following problems. Fill in the circle next to your choice. You may NOT use a calculator.

1. Estimate 43 × 18. The product is between which numbers?

    Ⓐ 30 and 80

    Ⓑ 100 and 150

    Ⓒ 300 and 800

    Ⓓ 1,000 and 1,500

Round 43 and 18 to the nearest 10 and multiply.

2. Estimate 29 × 11. The product is between which numbers?

    Ⓐ 30 and 80

    Ⓑ 100 and 150

    Ⓒ 300 and 800

    Ⓓ 1,000 and 1,500

Round both numbers to the nearest 10. Then use mental math to estimate the answer.

Estimating Division

You can also use rounding to estimate division. Note that when you divide one number into another, the number you get is called the **quotient**. Look at this problem:

Estimate 117 ÷ 9. The quotient is between which numbers?

    Ⓐ 0 and 5

    Ⓑ 5 and 10

    Ⓒ 10 and 20

    Ⓓ 20 and 30

To solve this problem, round 117 to 100. For this problem, it also helps to round 9 to 10. You know that 10 goes into 100 ten times, so answer choice C is correct.

Let's try another.

Estimate 550 ÷ 5. The quotient is between which numbers?

    Ⓐ 5 and 30

    Ⓑ 50 and 300

    Ⓒ 500 and 1,000

    Ⓓ 1,000 and 6,000

To estimate the quotient to this problem, round 550 to 600. Then divide 600 by 5 to get 120. Answer choice B is correct. Note that if you rounded 5 up to 10 before you divided, you would get the same range for your answer, which is 60. Finally, you might have been able to find the actual answer (110) by mental math, and that would help you to find the range, but usually estimation problems aren't easy to do by using mental math.

Practice Questions

Practice 11: Estimating Division

DIRECTIONS:

Choose the best of the answer choices given for each of the following problems. Fill in the circle next to your choice. You may NOT use a calculator.

1. **Estimate 148 ÷ 4. The quotient is between which numbers?**

    Ⓐ 0 and 5

    Ⓑ 5 and 20

    Ⓒ 20 and 40

    Ⓓ 40 and 60

Round 148 to 100. Then divide 100 by 4.

2. **Estimate 246 ÷ 6. The quotient is between which numbers?**

    Ⓐ 30 and 50

    Ⓑ 10 and 20

    Ⓒ 5 and 10

    Ⓓ 0 and 5

Round 246 to 200. About how many times does 6 go into 200? If you don't know, try rounding 6 to 5 and dividing.

Practice Questions

End-of-Chapter Practice Problems

DIRECTIONS:

Choose the best of the answer choices given for each of the following problems. Fill in the circle next to your choice. You may NOT use a calculator.

1. **Estimate 795 + 116. The sum is between which numbers?**

   Ⓐ 50 and 400

   Ⓑ 450 and 700

   Ⓒ 750 and 1,000

   Ⓓ 1,050 and 1,300

    Round 795 and 116 to the nearest 100 and add.

2. **Estimate 85 × 12. The product is between which numbers?**

   Ⓐ 30 and 80

   Ⓑ 100 and 150

   Ⓒ 300 and 800

   Ⓓ 900 and 1,500

    Round both 85 and 12 to the nearest 10.

3. **Estimate 252 ÷ 2. The quotient is between which numbers?**

   Ⓐ 10 and 30

   Ⓑ 100 and 300

   Ⓒ 1,000 and 3,000

   Ⓓ 10,000 and 30,000

HINT

Round 252 to the nearest 100 and divide by 2.

4. **Estimate 925 − 347. The difference is between which numbers?**

   Ⓐ 100 and 299

   Ⓑ 300 and 499

   Ⓒ 500 and 699

   Ⓓ 700 and 899

HINT

Round 925 and 347 to the nearest 100 and subtract.

5. **Estimate 372 + 108. The sum is between which numbers?**

   Ⓐ 50 and 400

   Ⓑ 450 and 700

   Ⓒ 750 and 1,000

   Ⓓ 1,050 and 1,300

HINT

Round 372 and 108 to the nearest 100 and add.

6. **Estimate 87 × 12. The product is between which numbers?**

   Ⓐ 30 and 80

   Ⓑ 100 and 150

   Ⓒ 300 and 800

   Ⓓ 900 and 1,200

Round 87 and 12 to the nearest 10 and multiply.

7. **Estimate 114 ÷ 6. The quotient is between which numbers?**

   Ⓐ 30 and 50

   Ⓑ 10 and 20

   Ⓒ 5 and 9

   Ⓓ 0 and 5

Round 114 to the nearest 100 and 6 to the nearest 10 and divide.

Chapter 4

Geometry

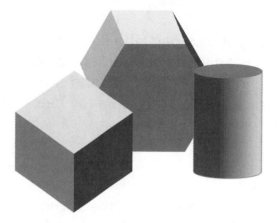

Shapes are formed by lines, and there are many different types of shapes. Shapes can be two- or three-dimensional. In this chapter, you'll learn about lines and shapes.

Lines

A **line** is straight and goes in two directions. To show that it continues in two different directions, a line has an arrow at each end. You can see a line below:

A **line segment** is part of a line. It is different from a line, because it has a beginning and an end. A point is used to show where a line segment begins and ends. This point is called an **endpoint**. Look at the line segment shown below. It has two endpoints.

A **ray** is also part of a line, but it is different from a line segment, because it has only one endpoint and one arrow. The arrow means that it keeps on going in one direction, and the endpoint means that it stops in the other direction. You can see a ray below. Notice that it has one endpoint and one arrow.

Parallel lines run in the **same direction**. They can be **vertical** (up and down), **horizontal** (side to side), or even at an angle (such as corner to corner), but they never cross each other.

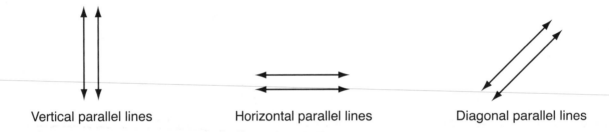

Vertical parallel lines   Horizontal parallel lines   Diagonal parallel lines

Perpendicular lines cross each other like the lines in a plus sign (+). They meet at a 90° angle. When lines cross, they are said to **intersect**. The place where lines intersect is called the **point of intersection**. Look at the perpendicular lines shown here:

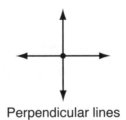

Perpendicular lines

Can you name each of the figures below? Write the name of the figure on the line beneath it.

1.

_____

2.

_____

3.

_____

4.

_____

5.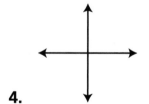

_____

Now fill in the blanks with the correct words.

6. **The points that show where a line segment begins and ends are called**

   _____.

7. **A _____ has an arrow at each end.**

8. **The point where two lines intersect is called the _____**

   _____.

You are correct if your answers are

1. a line segment

2. a ray

3. a line

4. perpendicular lines

5. parallel lines

6. endpoints

7. line

8. point of intersection

If you missed any of these, go back to the discussion of lines at the beginning of this chapter.

Practice Questions

Practice 12: Lines

DIRECTIONS:

Choose the best of the answer choices given for each of the following problems. Fill in the circle next to your choice.

1. **Which of these is a ray?**

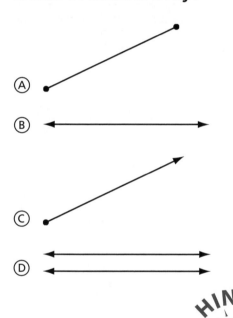

HINT

Remember that a ray does not have two arrows or two endpoints.

2. **What is point *A* called on the line segment *AB*?**

A   B

- Ⓐ point of intersection
- Ⓑ segment
- Ⓒ endpoint
- Ⓓ side

Review the section of this chapter on lines if you're not sure.

3. **What kind of lines are below?**

- Ⓐ rays
- Ⓑ parallel
- Ⓒ perpendicular
- Ⓓ endpoints

Review the section of this chapter on lines if you're not sure.

Angles

Two rays can make an **angle**. Look at the angle below. Each of the rays has an arrow at one end. The point where the rays meet is called the **vertex** of the angle. Each ray is called a **side** of the angle.

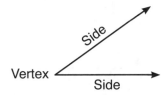

Angles are measured in **degrees**. A **protractor** is used to measure degrees. It is a lot like a ruler.

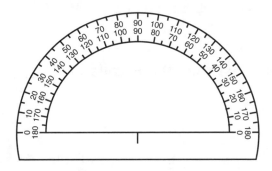

Angles have different names, depending on their measurement. A **right angle** measures exactly 90°. Look at the right angle below.

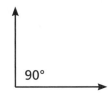

An **acute angle** measures less than 90°. It looks as if it is not open as much as a right angle. See the acute angle below? It measures 45°.

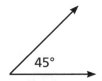

An **obtuse angle** measures more than 90°. It looks as if it is open more than a right angle. See the obtuse angle below? It measures 135°.

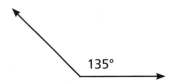

135°

Can you name each of the angles below?

1. An _____ angle has more than 90°.

2. An angle measuring less than 90° is called an _____ angle.

3. A _____ angle measures exactly 90°.

4. The point where two rays meet to form an angle is called the

   _____.

You are correct if your answers are:

1. obtuse
2. acute
3. right
4. vertex

If you missed any of these, review the section on angles in this chapter.

Practice Questions

Practice 13: Angles

DIRECTIONS:

Choose the best of the answer choices given for each of the following problems. Fill in the circle next to your choice.

1.   Which of the following shows an acute angle?

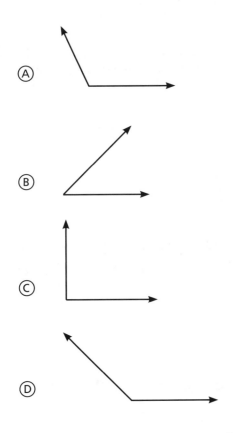

Ⓐ

Ⓑ

Ⓒ

Ⓓ

HINT

An acute angle measures less than 90°.

2. **Which of the following shows a right angle?**

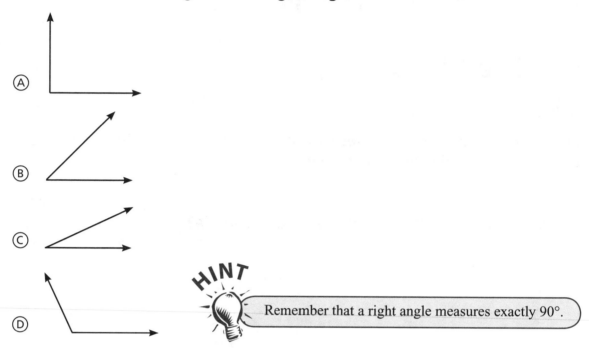

Ⓐ

Ⓑ

Ⓒ

Ⓓ

HINT

Remember that a right angle measures exactly 90°.

Two-Dimensional Shapes

Two-dimensional shapes are flat. They have a **length** and a **height**, but they don't have **depth**. Let's look at some typical two-dimensional shapes.

Circles

A **circle** is a round shape. All of the **points** on a circle are exactly the same distance from the **center** of the circle.

Center

Triangles

A **triangle** is a figure with three sides. Triangles come in different shapes and sizes. Their sides can be equal, but they don't have to be.

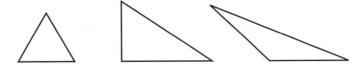

All triangles contain angles. A right triangle has one right angle:

Some triangles have one obtuse angle, which you learned is an angle larger than a right angle. These triangles are called obtuse triangles.

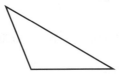

Quadrilaterals

A **quadrilateral** has four sides. Circles and triangles are not quadrilaterals. Rectangles and squares are quadrilaterals, because they have four sides.

A **rectangle** has two pairs of equal sides, and all angles are 90°. Rectangles can be different sizes, but two pairs of sides will always be equal.

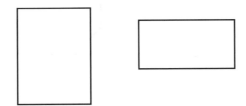

A **square** is a rectangle, with all four sides equal. Squares can be different sizes, but the sides are always equal.

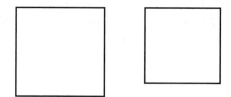

Other Two-Dimensional Shapes

A **pentagon** is a shape with five sides. These sides do not have to be equal.

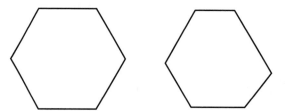

A **hexagon** is a shape with six sides. These sides do not have to be equal.

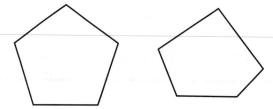

An **octagon** has eight sides. These sides do not have to be equal.

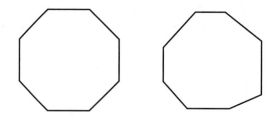

Look at the following two-dimensional shapes. Write what kind of shape each is on the line below it.

1.

_____

2.

_____

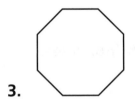

3.

_____

4.

_____

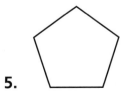

5.

_____

Now fill in the blanks with the correct words.

6. A _____ is a shape with six sides, and these sides do not have to be equal.

7. A _____ has four sides that are the same length, and all angles are 90°.

8. A _____ has four sides, four 90° angles, and the opposite sides are equal.

9. A _____ has three sides, and these sides do not have to be equal.

10. A _____ is any shape with four sides.

11. An _____ has eight sides, and these sides do not have to be equal.

12. A _____ has five sides, and these sides do not have to be equal.

You are correct if your answers are:

1. circle
2. square
3. octagon
4. rectangle
5. pentagon
6. hexagon
7. square
8. rectangle
9. triangle
10. quadrilateral
11. octagon
12. pentagon

If you missed one or more answers, review the section on two-dimensional shapes in this chapter.

Practice Questions

Practice 14: Two-Dimensional Shapes

DIRECTIONS:

Choose the best of the answer choices given for each of the following problems. Fill in the circle next to your choice.

1. **Which shape below is an octagon?**

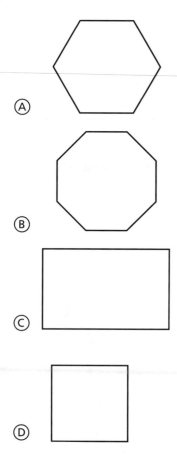

Ⓐ

Ⓑ

Ⓒ

Ⓓ

An octagon has eight sides that do not have to be equal.

2. Michi wrote the following riddle to her friend:

    I have two pairs of parallel sides. My angles all measure 90°. What am I?

    What is the answer to the riddle?

    Ⓐ triangle

    Ⓑ octagon

    Ⓒ rectangle

    Ⓓ circle

    HINT

    If you're not sure of this answer, go back and reread the section of this chapter that describes different kinds of shapes.

3. **Which of the following is a quadrilateral?**

    Ⓐ circle

    Ⓑ triangle

    Ⓒ hexagon

    Ⓓ square

    HINT

    Remember that a quadrilateral has four sides.

Three-Dimensional Shapes

Three-dimensional shapes look different from two-dimensional shapes, because they have **depth**, or a **width**. Three-dimensional shapes are sometimes called **solids**.

Look at the three-dimensional shape shown here. It is a **cube**. It looks like a square, but it has width. A cube looks like a block.

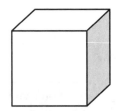

Notice that there are special names for parts of three-dimensional shapes. Each flat part on a three-dimensional shape is called a **face**. The lines in the shape are called **edges**, and the edges meet at **vertices**. (Vertices is the plural of **vertex**, or corner.) Each face on the cube is a shaped like a square. A cube has six faces and eight vertices.

Look at the **rectangular prism** below. It looks a lot like a box. Note that it also looks like a rectangle, except it has width. Like a square, a rectangular prism has six faces and eight vertices.

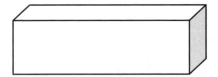

A **pyramid** looks a lot like a triangle. Its base can be a triangle or a quadrilateral, and it is often a square, as shown here. This pyramid has five faces and five vertices.

A **sphere** has no faces and no vertices. A sphere is a circle with depth. You can see from the figure below that it looks like a ball.

A **cone** looks just like an ice cream cone (see below). It has only one face and one vertex. The face is a circle.

A **cylinder** has a top face and a bottom face and no vertices. Both of its faces are circles. A can is an example of a cylinder, as can be seen below.

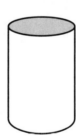

Look at each of the three-dimensional shapes below. Write what kind of shape each is on the line below it. Turn to the end of this exercise to check your answers.

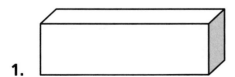

1.

_____

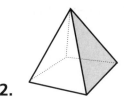

2. _____

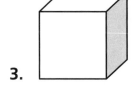

3. _____

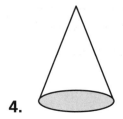

4. _____

5. _____

Now fill in the blanks with the correct words.

6. The flat part of a three-dimensional shape is called the _____

    _____.

7. The edges of a three-dimensional shape meet at _____

    _____.

8. A _____ is a three-dimensional shape with no faces.

9. A _____ looks like an ice cream cone.

10. The base of a _____ is often a square.

11. A _____ looks like a box.

Draw a line from each three-dimensional shape on the left to the two-dimensional shape it is most like on the right.

12. sphere   square

13. rectangular prism   triangle

14. pyramid   circle

15. cube   rectangle

You are correct if your answers are:

1. rectangular prism
2. pyramid
3. cube
4. cone
5. cylinder
6. face
7. corners, or vertices
8. sphere
9. cone
10. pyramid
11. rectangular prism (can be a cube but doesn't have to be)
12. sphere (circle)
13. rectangular prism (rectangle)
14. pyramid (triangle)
15. cube (square)

Practice Questions

Practice 15: Three-Dimensional Shapes

DIRECTIONS:

Choose the best of the answer choices given for each of the following problems. Fill in the circle next to your choice.

1. Which shape below is a sphere?

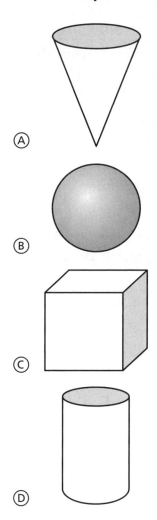

Ⓐ

Ⓑ

Ⓒ

Ⓓ

HINT

Remember that a sphere looks like a ball.

2. **Juan wrote the following riddle on the chalkboard:**

   I have 5 faces and 5 vertices, and I look like a triangle that has a square on the bottom. What am I?

   What is the answer to the riddle?

   Ⓐ   cone

   Ⓑ   cylinder

   Ⓒ   square pyramid

   Ⓓ   sphere

HINT

Think about a figure that looks like a triangle with a square on the bottom. What is this three-dimensional shape called? If you're not sure, turn back and review this section.

Congruent Shapes

Shapes that are the same size and same shape are called **congruent shapes**. Look at the rectangles below. These rectangles are congruent, because they are the same shape and size.

Now look at these triangles. They are **not** congruent.

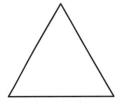
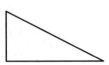

Practice Questions

Practice 16: Congruent Shapes

DIRECTIONS:

Choose the best of the answer choices given for each of the following problems. Fill in the circle next to your choice.

1. **Which of the following shows a pair of congruent figures?**

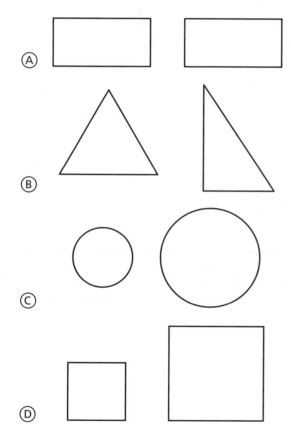

Choose the pair of shapes that is exactly the same.

2. **Which of the following shows a pair of figures that is NOT congruent?**

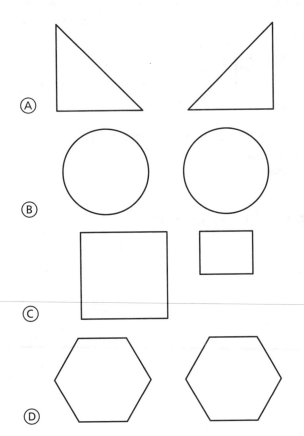

Ⓐ

Ⓑ

Ⓒ

Ⓓ

HINT

This time, you need to choose the shapes that are not exactly the same.

Perimeter

Add all the sides

The **perimeter** of a two-dimensional shape is the **sum** of all of the sides. The perimeter measures the distance around the object. To find the perimeter of most objects, you need to add the lengths of all the sides together.

Let's shade in the blocks that go around a pool to make the perimeter easier to find.

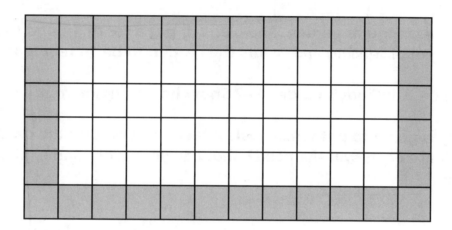

There are 12 block edges, or unit edges, on each of the two long sides of the pool. When you add them together, you get 24. There are unit edges along each of the two shorter sides of the pool. Adding those two together, you get 12. Now you need to add the sum of the two longer sides with the sum of the two shorter sides. 24 + 12 = 36. The perimeter of this pool is 36 units.

Now let's take a look at another object to find its perimeter. Suppose you have measured all of the sides of a triangle like the one below:

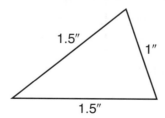

Using your ruler, you find that one side of the triangle measures 1 inches. Another side measures 1.5 inches. The last side also measures 1.5 inches.

To find the perimeter, you need to add all of these inches together as you did with the block edges around the pool. The perimeter of this triangle is 1 + 1.5 + 1.5 = 4 inches.

Sometimes you know the perimeter and either the length or width of an object, but you have to find the missing dimension.

For example, read this open-ended question:

Cindy has a rectangular garden. She plans to put a fence around the garden. She has 48 feet of fencing and wants the garden to be 14 feet long.

1.   **How wide will Cindy's garden be? Show how you got your answer.**

2.   **If Cindy is going to put fence posts 2 feet apart around the garden, how many fence posts will she need? Show all your work and explain your answer.**

It might help to draw a rectangle like the one shown here to answer this question.

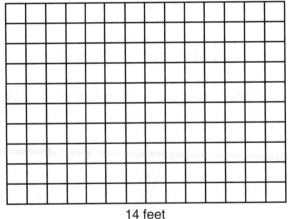

Perimeter = 48 feet

14 feet

You know that the length of the garden is 14 feet. Label both sides of the rectangle 14. You also know that Cindy has 48 feet of fencing, which will go around her garden. This is the perimeter of the garden. When you add the two sides that make up the lengths and the two sides that make up the widths, the total will be 48 feet. So, you know the length—two sides of the rectangle—equals 28 feet. When you subtract 28 from 48, you get 20. This is the total for the two sides that are the widths of the rectangle. If you divide 20 by 2, you get 10. Cindy's garden is 10 feet wide.

To answer the second part of the problem, divide 48 by 2, since Cindy plans to put a fence post every 2 feet. The answer is 24. Cindy will need 24 fence posts.

Area

Area measures the amount of space covered by a whole object. You saw that the perimeter measures the distance around an object. The area measures the space the entire object covers.

You can figure out the area of an object by counting all the blocks needed to cover it.

Look at the square below:

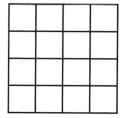

Count all of the blocks that cover the square. There are 16 blocks. So the amount of space that this square takes up is equal to 16 blocks. This could also be called 16 square units.

Let's try another example. Take a look at the rectangle-shaped pool from the exercise on perimeter.

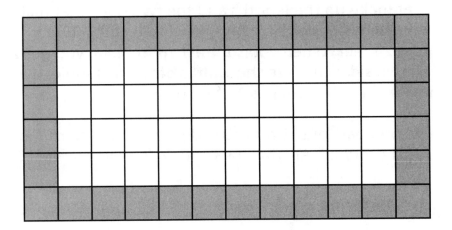

The length, or long side, of this rectangle is 12 units. The width, or short side, is 6 units. To find the area, multiply 12 times 6. The area is 72 square units.

Practice Questions

Practice 17: Perimeter and Area

DIRECTIONS:

Choose the best of the answer choices given for each of the following problems. Fill in the circle next to your choice.

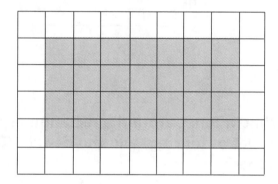

1. **What is the perimeter of the blue rectangle shown above?**

    Ⓐ 4

    Ⓑ 7

    Ⓒ 22

    Ⓓ 28

HINT

The perimeter is the distance around a shape. Use the block edges as an aid to count the distance around this rectangle. This is the perimeter. Remember to count the whole length and the whole width.

2. What is the area of the blue rectangle in problem 1?

    (A) 4

    (B) 7

    (C) 22

    (D) 28

When you are asked to find the area, multiply the length times the width. The answer represents square units.

3. Mr. Harmon is putting a fence around a rectangular deck in his backyard. He plans to use 36 feet of fencing, and the deck is 10 feet long. How wide is his deck in feet?

    (A) 2

    (B) 4

    (C) 6

    (D) 8

Add the two known sides of the deck. Subtract this number from the total length of fencing, and then divide the answer by 2.

Practice Questions

End-of-Chapter Practice Problems

DIRECTIONS:

Choose the best of the answer choices given for each of the following problems. Fill in the circle next to your choice.

1. Which triangle has an angle larger than a right angle?

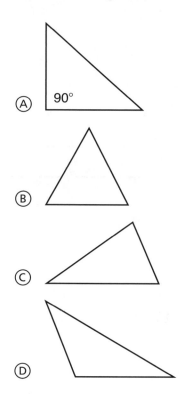

Ⓐ   90°

Ⓑ

Ⓒ

Ⓓ

HINT

Look at the triangle with the 90° angle marked. Choose a triangle that has an angle larger than this.

2. **What is the perimeter of the white rectangle shown below?**

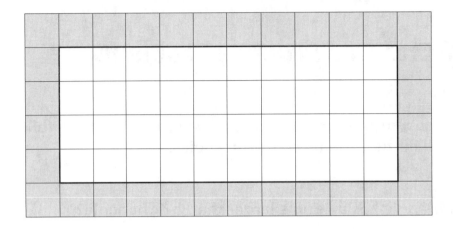

Ⓐ 20

Ⓑ 28

Ⓒ 30

Ⓓ 40

 Add up the lengths of all the sides of the rectangle.

3. **Max wrote the following riddle for his friend:**

I have 6 faces, 8 vertices, and I look like a box. What am I?

What is the answer to this riddle?

Ⓐ pyramid

Ⓑ cone

Ⓒ rectangular prism

Ⓓ sphere

 Begin by eliminating answer choices that you know are incorrect.

4. **Which angle below is an obtuse angle?**

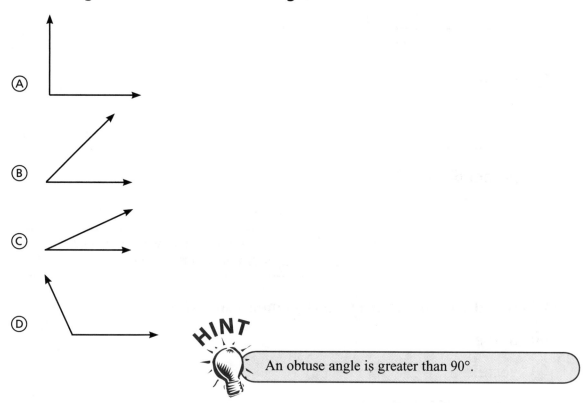

Ⓐ

Ⓑ

Ⓒ

Ⓓ

HINT

An obtuse angle is greater than 90°.

5. **Mrs. Garner wants to put up a wallpaper border in her living room. She needs 64 feet of border. The width of the room is 10 feet. What is the length of the room?**

Ⓐ 12 feet

Ⓑ 14 feet

Ⓒ 20 feet

Ⓓ 22 feet

HINT

Add the two widths of the room and subtract from 64 to get the total for the two lengths of the room. Remember to divide this by 2 to get the length.

6.   **What are these lines called?**

(A)   parallel lines

(B)   rays

(C)   line segments

(D)   perpendicular lines

HINT

If you can't remember what these lines are called, reread that part of the chapter.

7.   **What is the point where two rays meet called?**

(A)   angle

(B)   vertex

(C)   point of intersection

(D)   endpoint

HINT

If you don't know this answer, reread the section of the chapter about angles.

8.   **What is the name of a two-dimensional figure with six sides?**

(A)   sphere

(B)   pentagon

(C)   hexagon

(D)   rectangular prism

HINT

Eliminate answer choices that refer to three-dimensional figures.

Directions for the Open-Ended Question

The following question is an **open-ended** question. Remember to:

Read the question carefully and think about the answer.

Answer all the parts of the question.

Show your work or explain your answer.

You can answer the question by using words, tables, diagrams, OR pictures. You may use your calculator, ruler, and colored shapes.

9. **Look at the figures below.**

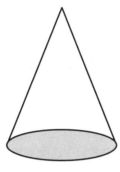 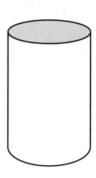

- **Name each figure.**
- **How many faces does each figure have?**
- **Write one way the figures are the same.**
- **Write one way the figures are different.**

_____

_____

_____

_____

Chapter 5

Measurement

Do you know how tall you are? If you do, it's because someone measured your height. Do you know how much you weigh? If you do, it's because someone weighed you. We measure many different things. We measure the food we eat. Some kinds of food are priced by how much they weigh. Others are priced by their capacity. Milk is often measured in gallons.

We also measure distance—how far apart things are. How far is your school from your home? You would probably measure this distance in miles. (Unless, of course, you live next door to the school; then you might measure the distance in feet or yards.)

You'll learn about two units of measurement in this chapter: the United States (U.S.) Customary unit of measurement (inches, feet, miles, ounces, pounds, quarts, and so on) and the metric system (centimeters, meters, kilometers, grams, kilograms, liters, and so on).

In this chapter, you'll learn about the different ways in which things can be measured.

Length (U.S. Customary Units)

How far is it to your best friend's home? How tall is a doorway? How long is a caterpillar? All of these questions can be answered by measuring distance. In this section of this chapter, you'll learn the U.S. Customary units for **distance**, or length.

Length is a kind of distance that refers to how long something is. You measure small objects by using **inches**. Have you ever have used a **ruler** before? If you have, you have probably seen inches marked off on a ruler. A **fraction of an inch** is a part of an inch. The lines that mark off inches on a ruler are usually longer than the other lines on a ruler. The smaller lines are used to indicate fractions of inches.

You would use inches to measure these things:

- the length of a pen or pencil

- the length of your finger

- the length of a feather

- the length of anything shorter than 12 inches

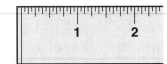

Most rulers measure up to 12 inches. Twelve inches equals one **foot**. A one-foot ruler is good to measure things like line segments. It is also good to measure anything that is just a few inches long.

But what do you use to measure things that are longer than 12 inches? If they aren't too long, you can use **feet** to do this. Do you know how tall you are? Your height is often measured in feet. Feet are also used to measure short distances. Longer rulers can have a few feet. Measuring tapes are many feet long.

You would use feet to measure these things:

- your height

- the length of a room

- the height of a doorway

You can also use yards to measure things that are longer than a couple of feet. People sometimes measure distances by using yards. There are three feet in a **yard**. Have you ever watched a football game? If you have, you might know that the distance the players run down the field is measured in yards. A U.S. football field is 100 yards long.

Yards can be used to measure these things:

- your street
- a swimming pool
- your classroom

Very large distances are measured in **miles**. There are 5,280 feet in every mile. Imagine that your school is 15 miles away. It is easier to say that your school is 15 miles away than to say it is 79,200 feet away!

Miles can be used to measure the distance between cities or faraway places.

Fill in the blank with the correct unit of measurement.

1. **The long lines on a ruler are used to measure** _____.

2. **Very long distances are measured in** _____.

3. **One yard equals three** _____.

4. **Twelve inches equals one** _____.

You are correct if your answers are:

1. inches

2. miles

3. feet

4. foot

If you missed one of these answers, go back to the last section, on U.S. Customary system for length.

Length (Metric System)

You read in the beginning of this chapter that the metric system is another method of measurement. Many people in other countries use the metric system to measure things. Some people in the United States also prefer to use the metric system.

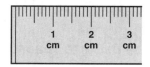

Centimeters are smaller than inches, so you would use them to measure small objects. Can you think of a small object that could be measured in centimeters? You could measure a leaf or a paper clip by using centimeters.

You could use centimeters to measure these things:

• your finger

• a feather

• a bee

Decimeters are the next largest unit of measurement. There are 10 centimeters in every decimeter. You might use decimeters to measure these things:

- wrapping paper

- cloth

There are 100 centimeters in a **meter**. A meter is a little longer than a yard (3 feet).

You might use meters to measure these things:

- your street

- a soccer field

- a swimming pool

- your classroom

To measure very long distances, you would use **kilometers**. There are 1,000 meters in one kilometer. If you wanted to measure the distance to your friend's house across town, you could measure it in kilometers.

Fill in the blank with the correct metric unit of measurement.

1. A _____ is a little longer than three feet.

2. A _____ is a unit used to measure small objects.

3. _____ are units used to measure very long distances.

4. There are 10 centimeters in a _____.

You are correct if your answers are:

1. meter

2. centimeter

3. kilometers

4. decimeter

If you missed any of these, review the section on metric units of length.

Practice Questions

Practice 18: Length

DIRECTIONS:

Choose the best of the answer choices given for each of the following problems. Fill in the circle next to your choice.

1. **What is the most reasonable estimate of the height of your bedroom ceiling?**

   Ⓐ 10 inches

   Ⓑ 8 feet

   Ⓒ 10 yards

   Ⓓ 8 miles

Think about the distance from your bedroom floor to the ceiling. Is it very small or very large? It is probably somewhere in the middle. Choose the answer that is somewhere in the middle that makes sense.

2. **What is the most reasonable estimate of the length of a penny?**

    Ⓐ 1.5 centimeters

    Ⓑ 1 decimeter

    Ⓒ 1.5 meters

    Ⓓ 1 kilometer

HINT

A penny is small. Make sure you pick a unit of measurement that is for something this small!

Weight (U.S. Customary Units)

When you go to the doctor, you get weighed on a scale. As you learned earlier, food is often sold according to how much it weighs. In this section, you'll learn about units of measurement for **weight**. Another word for weight is **mass**.

To measure very small items, we use **ounces**. Think of a regular slice of bread. It weighs about one ounce. There are 16 ounces in every **pound**. That means that 16 slices of bread weigh 1 pound.

We can use ounces to measure these things:

• a slice of bread

• a piece of chicken

• a potato

• a pencil or pen

• your shoe

We can use pounds to measure these things:

• your weight

• a sack of flour

• your desk

• a bag of topsoil

Tons are used to measure very large things. There are 2,000 pounds in one ton. Think of a car. An average car (not an SUV) weighs about $1\frac{1}{2}$ tons! That's really heavy!

You can use tons to measure these things:

• a boxcar of coal on a train

• a ship

• an elephant

Fill in the blank with the correct U.S. Customary unit of measurement.

1. **Your weight is measured in** _____.

2. **A slice of bread weighs about one** _____.

3. **There are 2,000 pounds in a** _____.

You are correct if your answers are:

1. pounds

2. ounce

3. ton

If you missed any of these, review the section on U.S. Customary units of weight.

Weight (Metric System)

Just like length, weight can also be measured by using metric units. **Grams** are used to tell the weight, or mass, of tiny objects. A paperclip weighs about one gram. That's very light!

You would use grams to measure these things:

- a postcard
- a pencil or pen
- spices

Kilograms are used to measure bigger things. One kilogram weighs a little more than two pounds. There are 1,000 grams in every kilogram.

You would use kilograms to measure these things:

- your weight
- a sack of flour
- your desk
- a piece of chicken

Metric tons are a lot like U.S. Customary tons. A metric ton is equal to 1,000 kilograms. You would use metric tons to measure these things:

- a car
- a ship
- an elephant

Complete this exercise about measuring weight by using metric units.

1. _____ are used to weigh very large objects.

2. **There are 1,000 grams in every _____.**

3. _____ are used to weigh things that are very small.

You are correct if your answers are:

1. Metric tons

2. kilogram

3. Grams

If you missed any of these, review the section on the metric system for weight.

Practice Questions

Practice 19: Weight

DIRECTIONS:

Choose the best of the answer choices given for each of the following problems. Fill in the circle next to your choice.

1.   **What is the most reasonable estimate of the weight of two cars?**

   Ⓐ   2 tons

   Ⓑ   2 pounds

   Ⓒ   2 ounces

   Ⓓ   2 grams

HINT

A car is very heavy. You need a large unit of measure to weigh it.

2. **A scale is used to weigh an object. The scale reads 1 gram. What object is most likely being weighed?**

   Ⓐ a potato

   Ⓑ a piece of lettuce

   Ⓒ a magazine

   Ⓓ a television

HINT

Remember, grams measure very light objects. Look at the answer choices and pick the lightest object.

Capacity (U.S. Customary Units)

The word **capacity** means how much substance, like a liquid, a container can hold. Capacity can also be measured by using U.S. Customary and metric units of measure.

Do you like to eat cereal with a teaspoon or a tablespoon? A **teaspoon** is a small spoon. There are 3 teaspoons in every **tablespoon**, which is a larger spoon.

A measuring **cup** holds 16 tablespoons of liquid. The next largest unit of measurement is a **pint**. There are two cups in every pint. The milk and juice cartons that come with most school lunches are measured in pints.

A **quart** is equal to 2 pints, or 4 cups, of liquid. Sometimes milk that you buy at a grocery store will come in a quart container.

Larger amounts of liquid, such as water, are usually measured in **gallons**. You can also buy a gallon of milk at the store; a gallon equals 4 quarts.

Complete this exercise about measuring capacity.

1. A _____ is equal to 3 teaspoons.

2. A _____ holds 16 tablespoons of liquid.

3. Large amounts of liquid are measured in _____.

4. A _____ equals 2 pints of liquid.

You are correct if your answers are:

1. tablespoon

2. cup

3. gallons

4. quart

If you missed any of these, review U.S. Customary units of capacity.

Capacity (Metric System)

A **liter** is about the same size as a quart. You might see milk or soft drinks sold in liter or two-liter containers. A **milliliter** is a very small amount, a thousandth of a liter, and is commonly used by a pharmacist or a doctor for measuring liquid medicines.

Complete this exercise about measuring capacity.

1. _____ are used to measure very small amounts of a liquid.

2. A _____ is about the same size as a quart.

You are correct if your answers are:

1. milliliter
2. liter

Practice Questions

Practice 20: Capacity

DIRECTIONS:

Choose the best of the answer choices given for each of the following problems. Fill in the circle next to your choice.

1. **What is the most reasonable estimate of the amount of liquid in a 2-cup thermos?**

    Ⓐ 1 pint

    Ⓑ 1 milliliter

    Ⓒ 1 quart

    Ⓓ 1 liter

HINT

If you don't know the answer to the question, reread the section on capacity. Find the unit of measurement that is about the same as a cup.

2. **What is the most reasonable estimate of the amount of water in a swimming pool?**

Ⓐ 80,000 cups

Ⓑ 80,000 pints

Ⓒ 80,000 quarts

Ⓓ 80,000 gallons

HINT

A swimming pool is pretty big! Remember that you will need a larger unit to measure the amount of water in a pool.

Measuring Time by Hours and Minutes

Measuring time involves telling the time it will be when something happens. For example, suppose it is 1:00 and you want to know what time it will be in two hours. It will be 3:00!

Most clocks with a standard clock face have both a "big" hand and a "little" hand. The big hand tells what minute it is, and the little hand tells what hour it is. Look at the clock below. The hours are printed on the inside of the clock, and the minutes are printed on the outside of the clock.

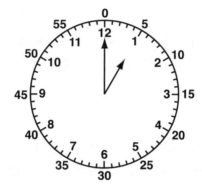

To tell the time, you look at the hour hand first and then the minute hand.

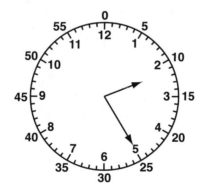

What time does this clock show? The hour hand, the little hand, is on the 2 and the minute hand, the big hand, is on the 25. It is 2:25.

Let's try another one.

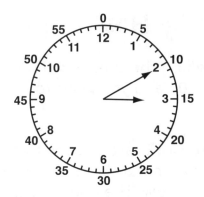

The hour hand, the little hand, is on the 3, and the minute hand, the big hand, is on the 10. It is 3:10.

The time from 12 noon until 11:59 at night is called P.M. The time from midnight until 11:59 in the morning is called A.M.

Read this problem.

Santina went to her friend's house at 3:00 P.M. Her mother told her to be home in 1 hour and 50 minutes. What time did Santina need to be home?

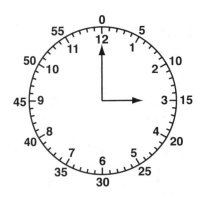

Ⓐ   3:50 P.M.

Ⓑ   4:40 P.M.

Ⓒ   4:50 P.M.

Ⓓ   5:00 P.M.

Did you get it right? If you add one hour to 3:00 P.M., it is 4:00 P.M. If you add another 50 minutes to this time, it is 4:50 P.M. Santina needed to be home by 4:50 P.M.

Practice Questions

Practice 21: Measuring Time by Hours and Minutes

DIRECTIONS:

Choose the best of the answer choices given for each of the following problems. Fill in the circle next to your choice.

1. Zack gets out of school at 2:30 P.M., as shown on the clock below. Then he goes to track practice for 1 hour and 15 minutes. What time does track practice end?

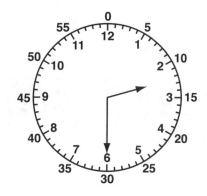

Ⓐ 2:45 P.M.

Ⓑ 3:00 P.M.

Ⓒ 3:15 P.M.

Ⓓ 3:45 P.M.

HINT

Add one hour to 2:30. Then add 15 minutes to this time.

2. **Christie has math class in the morning until 9:10 A.M., as shown on the clock below. After this, she goes to study hall for 30 minutes. What time does study hall end?**

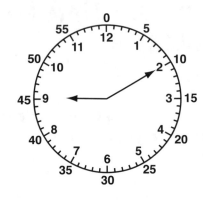

(A)   9:20 A.M.

(B)   9:30 A.M.

(C)   9:40 A.M.

(D)   9:50 A.M.

HINT

The hour doesn't change in this problem. Add 30 minutes to 10 minutes.

Measuring Time by Days and Weeks

To measure time in days and weeks, you use a **calendar**. You can plan your weekly schedule or count the number of weeks until a special event occurs.

A calendar is divided into 12 months. Each month shows the days of the week and the numerical dates for each day. For example, the calendar below shows the month of September. What day of the week does September 17 fall on? Find the box with the number 17. Then look up to the day of the week at the head of that column. The 17th falls on a Thursday.

September

Sun	Mon	Tue	Wed	Thu	Fri	Sat
		1	2	3	4	5
6	7	8	9	10	11	12
13	14	15	16	17	18	19
20	21	22	23	24	25	26
27	28	29	30			

Now let's try a problem. Use the calendar above in this problem.

Ernie broke his ankle. He had a cast put on it at the doctor's office on September 8. The doctor told Ernie to come back in exactly 2 weeks for a check-up. On what date will Ernie return to the doctor's office?

Ⓐ September 15

Ⓑ September 18

Ⓒ September 22

Ⓓ September 29

Did you get it right? To find the date two weeks after September 8, run your finger down the column from the box with the 8 to the box that is 2 rows down. The correct answer is September 22.

On what day of the week did Ernie go to the doctor's office? Run your finger up the column to the labels at the top. Both of Ernie's appointments were on a Tuesday.

Practice Questions

Practice 22: Measuring Time by Days and Weeks

DIRECTIONS:

Choose the best of the answer choices given for each of the following problems. Fill in the circle next to your choice.

1. Jackson Elementary School will hold a carnival on April 9. On what day of the week will the carnival be?

April

Sun	Mon	Tue	Wed	Thu	Fri	Sat
				1	2	3
4	5	6	7	8	9	10
11	12	13	14	15	16	17
18	19	20	21	22	23	24
25	26	27	28	29	30	

Ⓐ Monday

Ⓑ Wednesday

Ⓒ Friday

Ⓓ Saturday

HINT

Find the box on the calendar with the number 9. Then look up to the label at the top of the column.

2. Use the same calendar for this problem. Joan goes to a drawing class
    every Saturday. How many times will she attend the class in the month
    of April?

    (A) 3

    (B) 4

    (C) 5

    (D) 6

Find the column for Saturday. How many boxes in
this column have numbers?

Practice Questions

End-of-Chapter Practice Problems

DIRECTIONS:

Choose the best of the answer choices given for each of the following problems. Fill in the circle next to your choice.

1. **What is the most reasonable estimate of the weight of a truck?**

   Ⓐ 30 ounces

   Ⓑ 30 pounds

   Ⓒ 300 pounds

   Ⓓ 3 tons

HINT

Remember that a truck is very heavy.

2. **What unit of measure would be best to measure the length of a sidewalk in front of a house?**

   Ⓐ inches

   Ⓑ centimeters

   Ⓒ meters

   Ⓓ kilometers

HINT

Choose a unit of measurement that is not extremely small or extremely large.

3. On Saturday, Alicia finishes doing her chores at 9:30 A.M, as shown on the clock below. After this, she can go outside and play for 1 hour and 30 minutes. What time does she need to return home?

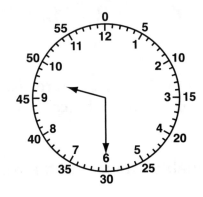

Ⓐ 10:00 A.M.

Ⓑ 10:30 A.M.

Ⓒ 11:00 A.M.

Ⓓ 11:30 A.M.

HINT

Remember that 30 minutes plus 30 minutes is 1 hour.

4. Which of the following is the smallest unit to measure an amount of liquid?

Ⓐ milliliter

Ⓑ gallon

Ⓒ liter

Ⓓ quart

HINT

Remember what measurement doctors and pharmacists use to measure small amounts.

5. **Gaylene wants to host a party for her tumbling team on a Saturday in January. Which of the following dates should she choose?**

January

Sun	Mon	Tue	Wed	Thu	Fri	Sat
				1	2	3
4	5	6	7	8	9	10
11	12	13	14	15	16	17
18	19	20	21	22	23	24
25	26	27	28	29	30	31

Ⓐ January 9

Ⓑ January 17

Ⓒ January 25

Ⓓ January 30

HINT

Find the column of boxes under the heading for Saturday. Which date is in that column?

Chapter 6

Algebra

In mathematics, patterns are everywhere. The study of patterns and relations is called **algebra**. If you count by twos—2, 4, 6, 8, and 10—you are using a pattern. If you count by threes or fours, you're also using a pattern. Some patterns stop eventually, and others keep on going, sometimes in more than one direction. You'll learn about patterns in this chapter.

You'll also learn about functions in this chapter. A **function** is a kind of pattern. Functions can be used to find the missing value in a number sentence—for example, to find what belongs in the box in a sentence such as $3 \times \square = 0$. The **associative** and **commutative properties** help to find missing values. You'll also learn about these properties in this chapter.

Patterns

If a group of numbers has a pattern, you can usually tell what number comes next. Patterns that keep on going are called continuous. These patterns usually have three dots at the end. These three dots are called ellipses (ee-LIP-seez). Look at the numbers on the next page.

1, 5, 9, 13, 17 . . .

The pattern above is a **numeric pattern**. The ellipses (series of dots) at the end mean that the pattern keeps on going. Look for a pattern in these numbers. Do they get larger or smaller? They get larger. What do you have to add to each number to get the next number?

$$1 + 4 = 5$$
$$5 + 4 = 9$$
$$9 + 4 = 13$$
$$13 + 4 = 17$$

You add 4 to each number to get the next number. So the next number is 21. Another way to create this pattern is to start at 1 and skip-count by 4's.

Now look at this pattern:

100, 96, 92, 88, 84 . . .

For this pattern, you subtract 4 from each number to get the next number, so the next number is 80.

Now look at this group of numbers:

2, 4, 6, 8, 2, 4, 6, 8 . . .

These numbers are a **repeating pattern**. Can you see that the next number is a 2? In fact, can you see that the next five numbers are 2, 4, 6, 8, 2? So sometimes a pattern involves repetition, not just changing each number by some operation, such as addition, subtraction, multiplication, or division.

Repeating patterns can also be made with shapes or symbols. This kind of pattern is called a **geometric pattern**. Look at this pattern.

What are the next two shapes in this pattern? Draw them on the line below.

Did you draw a triangle and a triangle? If so, you are correct. The complete pattern is circle, triangle, triangle, square.

Practice Questions

Practice 23: Patterns

DIRECTIONS:

Choose the best of the answer choices given for each of the following problems. Fill in the circle next to your choice.

1. **Which rule is assigned to these numbers?**

    6, 14, 22, 30, 38, 46 . . .

    Ⓐ Add 4

    Ⓑ Add 6

    Ⓒ Add 8

    Ⓓ Add 10

HINT

Look at the numbers as they get larger. What is added to each number to get the next one?

2. **Which rule is assigned to these numbers?**

$$52, 49, 46, 43, 40, 37, 34, 31 \ldots$$

Ⓐ Subtract 2

Ⓑ Subtract 3

Ⓒ Subtract 4

Ⓓ Subtract 5

HINT

Figure out by finding how much the numbers are decreasing.

3. **What are the next two shapes in the pattern below?**

Ⓐ

Ⓑ

Ⓒ

Ⓓ

HINT

Look for the place where the pattern starts to repeat itself. Then you can figure out which two shapes follow the square in the pattern.

Functions

A **function** is a kind of pattern. A **function machine** is an imaginary machine you can use to help you determine a pattern. You put a number into the machine. Then another number is added to, subtracted from, multiplied by, or divided into this number, and a new number comes out of the machine. The numbers you put into the machine are called input. The numbers that come out of the machine are called output. A table of numbers under the function machine helps you to determine the pattern. Look at the function machine below:

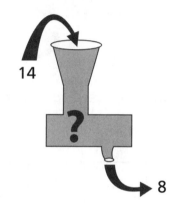

Input	14	8	10	12
Output	8	2	4	?

Can you figure out the missing number in the table? All of the numbers in the table have 6 subtracted from them. The number 6 subtracted from 12 is 6. The missing number is 6, because $12 - 6 = 6$.

Let's try another problem, but one that has two function machines.

When 7 is dropped into the first function machine, it comes out as 5. When 5 is dropped into the second function machine, it comes out as 10. The tables for both function machines are shown below. What happens to 11 if it goes through both function machines?

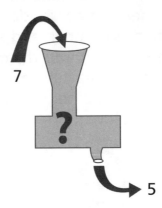

The following table shows some other input and output data for the first machine.

Input	7	10	6	11
Output	5	8	4	?

The second function machine operates as follows:

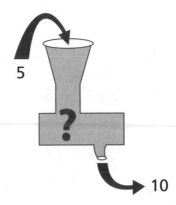

The table shows some other input and output data for the second machine.

Input	5	8	4	☐
Output	10	13	9	?

- Ⓐ 14
- Ⓑ 11
- Ⓒ 9
- Ⓓ 4

First you have to find the missing number in the first table so you can insert it into the second machine. Did you figure out the pattern for the first function machine? The number 2 is subtracted from each of the input numbers to get the output number. So if the number 11 is input, 9 will be the output number.

Now look at the second table. The output from the last table is now the input. What happens to the numbers in this table? They each get larger by 5. To find the missing number in this table, you have to add 5 to 9. The missing number is 14, so the correct answer choice is A.

Practice Questions

Practice 24: Functions

DIRECTIONS:

Choose the best of the answer choices given for each of the following problems. Fill in the circle next to your choice.

1.   When 9 is dropped into this function machine, it comes out as 18.

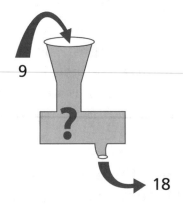

Input	9	7	11	12
Output	18	16	20	?

What does 12 come out as when it is dropped into the function machine?

Ⓐ   4

Ⓑ   21

Ⓒ   20

Ⓓ   22

Think about what is happening to each of the numbers. Are they getting larger? By how much?

2. **When 13 is dropped into this function machine, it comes out as 10.**

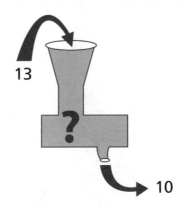

13

10

The following table shows some other input and output data for the machine.

Input	13	7	15	9
Output	10	4	12	?

What is the missing number in the table?

(A) 5

(B) 6

(C) 7

(D) 8

HINT

Figure out how much is subtracted from each of the numbers in the input row of the table to get the numbers in the output row.

3. When 4 is dropped into the first of two machines, it comes out as 9.
    When 9 is dropped into the second machine, it comes out as 12.

    For the first machine:

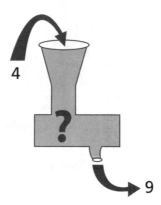

4

9

    The table below shows some other input and output data for the first
    machine.

Input	4	6	3	7
Output	9	11	8	?

    For the second machine:

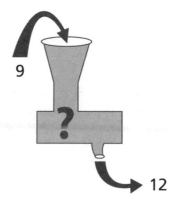

9

12

The table below shows some other input and output data for the second machine.

Input	9	11	8	□
Output	12	14	11	?

What is the output number for 7 when it is dropped into the first machine?

Ⓐ 10

Ⓑ 11

Ⓒ 12

Ⓓ 13

Don't get confused by the two tables. Just look at the first table to answer this question.

4. If the output from the first function machine is input into the second function machine from problem 3, what is the missing output value on the table for the second machine?

Ⓐ 9

Ⓑ 10

Ⓒ 14

Ⓓ 15

The numbers in this table increase. Figure out what is added to each number in the input row to get the number in the output row.

Input/Output Tables and T-Charts

Input/output tables and **T-charts** are very similar to the function machines and the tables beneath the function machines. Look at the problem for the input/output table below:

What number is missing in the output column of the table below?

Input	Output
2	9
3	10
4	?
5	12

Ⓐ   7

Ⓑ   8

Ⓒ   10

Ⓓ   11

To answer this question, look closely at the first number in the input column and the first number in the output column. What do you have to do to the number 2 to make it 9? You add 7. Look at the second number. What do you have to do to the number 3 to make it 10? Once again, you add 7. The missing number is 7 more than 4, or 11. So answer choice D is correct.

A **T-chart** is just like an input/output table, but it is set up in a different way. Look at the T-chart below:

x	y
14	9
12	7
9	4
8	3

Which rule is assigned to the *x* column in order to get the number in the *y* column?

- Ⓐ Add 5
- Ⓑ Subtract 5
- Ⓒ Multiply by 3
- Ⓓ Divide by 3

To answer this question, look closely at the first number in the *x* column. It's 14. What do you have to do to 14 to get 9? You have to subtract 5. If you look at all of the numbers in the *x* column, you'll see that you have to subtract 5 from each of them to get the number in the *y* column. Answer choice B is correct.

Practice Questions

Practice 25: Input/Output Tables and T-Charts

DIRECTIONS:

Choose the best of the answer choices given for each of the following problems. Fill in the circle next to your choice.

1. **What is the missing number in the table below?**

Input	Output
6	12
8	14
10	16
12	?

Ⓐ 6

Ⓑ 8

Ⓒ 14

Ⓓ 18

Be sure to look at all of the numbers in the input/ output table before making a decision about the rule.

2. **Which rule is assigned to the numbers in the *x* column to get the numbers in the *y* column?**

x	y
9	18
8	16
7	14
6	12

Ⓐ Add 9

Ⓑ Subtract 9

Ⓒ Multiply by 2

Ⓓ Divide by 2

HINT

Notice that the numbers in the *y* column are larger. This means addition or multiplication was used.

Other Kinds of Patterns

Patterns can also relate to an activity. Look at this problem:

Pedro does a different type of exercise each day, according to this pattern:

Day 1:	Walks
Day 2:	Rides bike
Day 3:	Jogs
Day 4:	Plays basketball
Day 5:	Walks
Day 6:	Rides bike
Day 7:	Jogs
Day 8:	Plays basketball

What kind of exercise will Pedro do on Day 9?

Did you say that he will walk? That's great! Now, what kind of exercise will Pedro do on Day 22? Answering this question is harder. But you can figure it out by repeating the pattern, as shown below:

Day 1:	Walks
Day 2:	Rides bike
Day 3:	Jogs
Day 4:	Plays basketball
Day 5:	Walks
Day 6:	Rides bike

Day 7:	Jogs
Day 8:	Plays basketball
Day 9:	Walks
Day 10:	Rides bike
Day 11:	Jogs
Day 12:	Plays basketball
Day 13:	Walks
Day 14:	Rides bike
Day 15:	Jogs
Day 16:	Plays basketball
Day 17:	Walks
Day 18:	Rides bike
Day 19:	Jogs
Day 20:	Plays basketball
Day 21:	Walks
Day 22:	Rides bike

You can see from the pattern that Pedro will ride a bike on the 22nd day.

Let's try a different problem.

You are trying to save money to buy a gift for your mother's birthday. You record in the chart below the total amount of money you have at the end of each week.

Week	1	2	3	4	5
Total amount of money saved	$2.75	$5.50	$8.25	$11.00	

If you continue saving money following this pattern, how much money will you have at the end of Week 5?

   Ⓐ $8.25

   Ⓑ $11.75

   Ⓒ $13.75

   Ⓓ $14.75

To solve this problem, begin by subtracting $2.75 from $5.50. The answer is $2.75. Now add $2.75 to $5.50. If you do this, you get the amount of money in Week 3. If you keep on going, you'll see that the pattern is to add $2.75 each week. So you can figure out how much money you will have saved in Week 5 by adding $2.75 to $11.00, the amount of money you have in Week 4. The answer is $13.75, choice C.

Practice Questions

Practice 26: Other Kinds of Patterns

DIRECTIONS:

Choose the best of the answer choices given for each of the following problems. Fill in the circle next to your choice.

1. **Tammy's grandmother makes a different kind of food each day, according to this pattern:**

Day 1:	Meatloaf
Day 2:	Chicken
Day 3:	Spaghetti
Day 4:	Sandwiches
Day 5:	Fish
Day 6:	Meatloaf
Day 7:	Chicken
Day 8:	Spaghetti
Day 9:	Sandwiches
Day 10:	Fish

What food will Tammy's grandmother make on Day 16?

Ⓐ Meatloaf

Ⓑ Chicken

Ⓒ Spaghetti

Ⓓ Sandwiches

HINT

Notice that there are 5 days to the pattern. Repeat the pattern to Day 16.

Directions for the Open-Ended Question

The following question is an open-ended question. Remember to:

Read the question carefully and think about the answer.

Answer all the parts of the question.

Show your work or explain your answer.

2. You are saving the money you make for **babysitting your little brother.
    You record the total amount of money you have at the end of each
    week in the chart below.**

Week	1	2	3	4	5
Total amount of money saved	$5.50	$8.75	$12.00	$15.25	

*   **If you continue saving money following this pattern, how much
    money will you have at the end of Week 5? Explain the pattern you
    used to get your answer.**

*   **A clock radio you would like to buy costs $20.00. How many weeks
    will it take you to save at least that much money? Show your work or
    explain your answer.**

Open Sentences

Some questions require you to fill in the blank with the correct number. These are called **open sentences**. Look at this open sentence:

14 ÷ 2 = ☐

You can probably solve this problem by using mental math. You might already know that 14 divided by 2 is 7.

Let's try another.

If 24 − ☐ = 10, then what is the value of ☐?

This one is more difficult. To solve this one, you need to think, "What number subtracted from 24 gives 10?" The number is 14, because 24 − 14 = 10.

You can also **reverse** open sentences of this type. Can you see that the missing number is the difference between 24 and 10? You can reverse subtraction and division problems, so that 24 − ☐ = 10 becomes 24 − 10 = ☐.

An example using division is 12 ÷ ☐ = 6, which reverses to 12 ÷ 6 = ☐. Of course, you might already have used mental math to get the correct answer, 2. Note that reversing does NOT work for addition or multiplication problems.

Sometimes a letter is used in place of the box, and you have to figure out the value of this letter. Look at this open sentence:

n **= 21 ÷ 3**

To solve for *n*, divide 3 into 21.

By using mental math, we see that 21 ÷ 3 = 7. Therefore, 7 = 21 ÷ 3, and *n* is 7.

Let's try one more:

18 − x = 10

By reversing the open sentence, we see that 18 − 10 = x, so x is 8. You may have gotten this answer by mental math as well.

Now substitute 8 in the original open sentence to make sure you have the correct answer: 18 − 8 = 10. It works!

Solve each of the following open sentences.

1. 2 × 6 = ☐

2. 15 + ☐ = 32

3. 54 − x = 24

4. 15 + 9 = n

5. 32 − x = 18

You are correct if your answers are:

1. 2 × 6 = 12
2. 15 + 17 = 32
3. 54 − 30 = 24
4. 15 + 9 = 24
5. 32 − 14 = 18

If you missed any of these, review the section on open sentences.

Practice Questions

Practice 27: Open Sentences

DIRECTIONS:

Choose the best of the answer choices given for each of the following problems. Fill in the circle next to your choice.

1. If 96 ÷ ☐ = 12, what is the value of ☐?

    Ⓐ 7

    Ⓑ 8

    Ⓒ 9

    Ⓓ 11

HINT

Reverse the equation and divide 12 into 96.

2. If 72 − ☐ = 38, then what is the value of ☐?

    Ⓐ 28

    Ⓑ 30

    Ⓒ 32

    Ⓓ 34

HINT

Reverse the equation and subtract 38 from 72.

3. What does the *n* equal in 50 × *n* = 150?

    (A)   1

    (B)   2

    (C)   3

    (D)   4

HINT

Think: 50 times what number gives 150?

4. If 144 ÷ ☐ = 12, then what is the value of ☐?

    (A)   8

    (B)   10

    (C)   12

    (D)   14

HINT

Reverse the equation and divide 12 into 144.

Equations and Inequalities

You can use open sentences to compare numbers. These kind of open sentences are called **equations and inequalities**. They use the following signs: = (equal to), > (greater than), and < (less than).

Look at this open sentence: $\square$ = 47

What number belongs in the box? The number must be equal to 47. Thus, the answer is 47.

Now try this problem.

Jackie wrote the number sentence below.

$112 < \square$

Which number can replace the box to make the number sentence correct?

    (A)   110

    (B)   111

    (C)   112

    (D)   113

The number sentence says "112 is less than some number." Look for the answer that is **greater** than 112. Choices A and B are less than 112. Choice C is equal to 112. Only Choice D is correct. 112 < 113 is a true statement.

You can also solve equations and inequalities that have symbols or shapes in place of numbers. Look at this problem.

Cooper wrote the open sentences below.

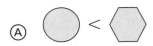

If both of Cooper's open sentences are true, which open sentence is also true?

Ⓐ ◯ < ⬡

Ⓑ ◯ > ⬡

Ⓒ △ < ◯

Ⓓ △ > ⬡

To solve the problem, check each open sentence to see if it is true. Choice A is true, because the circle has to be less than the hexagon. Choice B is not true, because the circle is not greater than the hexagon. Choice C is not true because the triangle is greater than the circle, not less than. Choice D is not true, because the triangle is less than the hexagon, not greater than. So the only true open sentence among the answers is A.

Practice Questions

Practice 28: Equations and Inequalities

DIRECTIONS:

Choose the best of the answer choices given for each of the following problems. Fill in the circle next to your choice.

1. Darnell wrote the open sentence below.

   $$173 = \square$$

   Which number can replace the box to make the number sentence correct?

   Ⓐ 0

   Ⓑ 1

   Ⓒ 172

   Ⓓ 173

 The answer must be equal to 173.

2. Which number can replace the box to make this number sentence correct?

   $$846 < \square$$

   Ⓐ 847

   Ⓑ 846

   Ⓒ 845

   Ⓓ 844

 Remember that the "<" sign means "less than."

3. **Look at the open sentences below.**

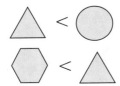

If both of these open sentences are true, which open sentence is also true?

Ⓐ △ < ⬡

Ⓑ △ > ◯

Ⓒ ◯ > ⬡

Ⓓ ◯ < ⬡

HINT

Check each open sentence in the answers against the first two open sentences. For example, can the triangle be less than the hexagon?

Number Sentences

You can use open sentences to answer problems given in words, or **number sentences**.

Look at this problem:

Jennifer had 32 pencils. She gave some to her little sister, and now Jennifer has 20. Which number sentence could you use to find out how many pencils Jennifer gave her sister?

Ⓐ $20 - \square = 32$

Ⓑ $20 \times \square = 32$

Ⓒ $20 + 32 = \square$

Ⓓ $32 - 20 = \square$

For this problem, you have to find the answer choice that you could use to find out how many pencils Jennifer gave away. Answer choice A isn't correct. Subtracting a number from 20 won't tell you how many pencils she gave away. Answer choice B isn't correct either. You wouldn't multiply to find out how many pencils she gave away; you would subtract. Adding 20 and 32 (answer choice C) would give you a large number. This number wouldn't tell you how many pencils Jennifer gave away. But if you subtract 20 from 32, as in answer choice D, you would find out how many pencils she gave away. Jennifer gave away 12 pencils.

Practice Questions

Practice 29: Number Sentences

DIRECTIONS:

Choose the best of the answer choices given for each of the following problems. Fill in the circle next to your choice.

1. Peter had 24 crayons. His mother gave him more crayons. He now has 36 crayons. Which number sentence could you use to find out how many crayons his mother gave him?

   Ⓐ $24 + 36 = \square$

   Ⓑ $36 - 24 = \square$

   Ⓒ $24 \times \square = 36$

   Ⓓ $\square + 26 = 24$

   HINT

   The number of crayons Peter's mother gave him is the difference between what he has now and what he had before.

2. Tara has 68 marbles. She gives 24 marbles to her friend. Which number sentence could you use to find out how many marbles Tara has now?

   Ⓐ $68 + 24 = \square$

   Ⓑ $\square \times 24 = 68$

   Ⓒ $68 - 24 = \square$

   Ⓓ $24 - \square = 68$

   HINT

   Tara started with 68 and gave 24 away, so she has fewer now.

Practice Questions

End-of-Chapter Practice Problems

DIRECTIONS:

Choose the best of the answer choices given for each of the following problems. Fill in the circle next to your choice.

1. When 14 is dropped into this machine, it comes out as 4.

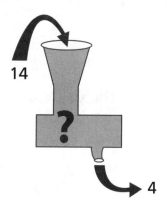

Input	14	12	38	11	28
Output	4	2	28	1	?

What is the missing number in the table?

Ⓐ 2

Ⓑ 8

Ⓒ 10

Ⓓ 18

Notice that the machine makes the numbers small, so the function involves subtraction or division.

2. **Which rule is assigned to these numbers?**

    5, 14, 23, 32, 41, 50, . . .

    Ⓐ Add 7

    Ⓑ Add 8

    Ⓒ Add 9

    Ⓓ Add 11

 Figure out the difference between the numbers.

3. **If 36 ÷ ☐ = 3, then what is the value of ☐?**

    Ⓐ 16

    Ⓑ 14

    Ⓒ 12

    Ⓓ 8

 This is division, so you can reverse the equation.

4. **Which rule is assigned to the *x* column in order to get the number in the *y* column?**

x	y
18	12
17	11
15	9
10	4

Ⓐ Add 6

Ⓑ Subtract 6

Ⓒ Multiply by 3

Ⓓ Divide by 3

HINT

Notice that the numbers in the *y* column are smaller than the numbers in the *x* column, so the rule should involve subtraction or division.

5. **Which number can replace the box to make this number sentence correct?**

54 > ☐

Ⓐ 56

Ⓑ 55

Ⓒ 54

Ⓓ 53

HINT

Remember that the ">" sign means "greater than."

6. Brenda's class has 24 students. Brenda's teacher asks her to give each student two juice boxes. Which number sentence could be used to find out how many juice boxes Brenda needs?

Ⓐ $24 \times 2 = \square$

Ⓑ $24 \div 2 = \square$

Ⓒ $\square + 2 = 24$

Ⓓ $2 - \square = 24$

Think about what must be done to the number 24 if each of the 24 students gets two juice boxes.

7. What are the next two shapes in the pattern below?

 **? ?**

Ⓐ △ ◯

Ⓑ ◯ △

Ⓒ ▢ ◯

Ⓓ △ ▢

The complete pattern is made up of four shapes.

Chapter 7

Statistics and Probability

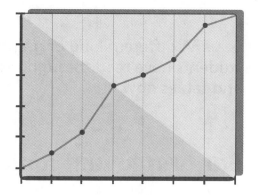

Suppose you would like to find out what kind of music most of the students in your class listen to. You grab a pencil and paper and ask each student in your class about his or her favorite music, and then you write down their answers. You use this information to reach this conclusion: Most of the students in your class like pop music!

The information you wrote down is called **data** or **statistics**. People use data in many different ways. The weatherperson on your television gathers data to make a prediction about the weather.

Your math teacher might give the students in your class a quiz. If the students do not do well on the quiz, your teacher might decide to spend more time teaching the lesson. The quiz your teacher gave was to gather data, or information, about whether your class understood the lesson. In this chapter, you'll learn how to reach a conclusion or make a prediction based on data.

Using Data

Data points are often displayed in **graphs** and **tables**. A graph might be used to show how many students played a certain sport over the past five years. A different kind of graph might be used to show how many books students have read throughout the year. Let's review some common graphs and tables now.

Bar Graphs and Tables

A **bar graph** uses bars to show data. These bars are most often **vertical** (up and down), but they can also be **horizontal** (side to side). Often the bars on a bar graph will be printed in different colors, but on the NY State Mathematics test, the bars will be gray. Look at the bar graph shown below:

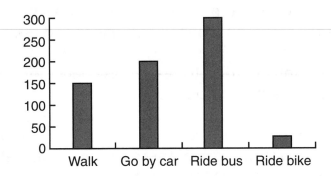

How Students Get to School

This bar graph shows how students get to school. The different ways they get to school are listed on the bottom of the graph—walk, go by car, ride the bus, and ride by bike. The numbers of students are listed on the side—0, 50, 100, and so on—and the value of each bar is determined by its height. You can use this bar graph to tell how many students get to school each way.

The same information can be presented in a **table**. Like the bar graph, the table has a title. Each column has a heading that explains what it contains. Look at the table on the next page.

Ways Students Get to School

How They Travel	Number of Students
walk	150
car ride	
bus ride	
ride bike	

Read the bar graph to fill in the rest of the table.

Did you write the correct numbers? If you wrote that 200 students get a car ride, 300 ride the bus, and 25 ride bikes, you are right. If any of your answers were incorrect, look more carefully at the values of the bars in the bar graph.

Notice that most students get to school by bus. You can learn new facts by studying graphics such as bar graphs and tables.

Pictographs

In a **pictograph,** another kind of graph, **pictures** stand for data. A picture often stands for more than one of an item. You have to look at a key to see how many things a picture stands for. Look at this pictograph. It shows how many magazines students collected for recycling during the school year:

Number of Magazines Collected for Recycling During the School Year

Caleb	
Martin	
Katelyn	
Rose	

Key ▯ = 10 magazines

Use the pictograph and the key to tell how many magazines each friend collected. Notice that each ▯ is equal to 10 magazines. So, ▯ is equal to 5 magazines. The first one is done for you.

Caleb:	100 magazines
Martin:	_____
Katelyn:	_____
Rose:	_____

Who collected the most magazines? _____

If you wrote that Martin collected 155 magazines, Katelyn collected 125 magazines, and Rose collected 85 magazines, you are right. Martin collected the most magazines. If any of your answers were incorrect, recheck your multiplication. Remember that  is equal to 5 magazines.

Practice Questions

Practice 30: Using Data and Graphs

DIRECTIONS:

Choose the best of the answer choices given for each of the following problems. Fill in the circle next to your choice.

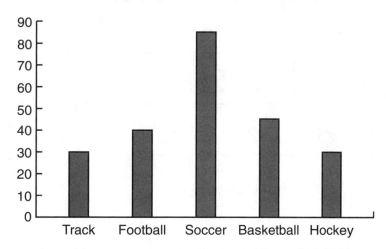

Kinds of Sports Students Play

1. **According to the bar graph above, how many students play football?**

    Ⓐ 20

    Ⓑ 30

    Ⓒ 40

    Ⓓ 50

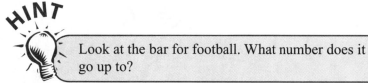

Look at the bar for football. What number does it go up to?

2. **Which sport do most students play?**

Ⓐ Track

Ⓑ Football

Ⓒ Soccer

Ⓓ Basketball

HINT

Choose the sport with the highest bar.

3. **Lawrence did a survey of his classmates' reading for two months.**

Number of Books Read

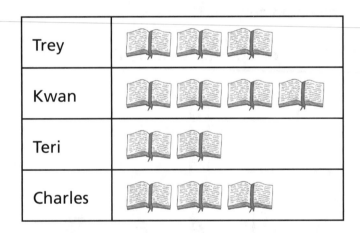

Trey	
Kwan	
Teri	
Charles	

Key: 📖 = 3 books

What was the largest number of books read by any of these students?

Ⓐ 12

Ⓑ 15

Ⓒ 9

Ⓓ 6

HINT

Look at the key to see how many books each book symbol stands for.

Line Graphs

A **line graph** shows the relationship between two things. If the first gets larger or smaller, it affects the second. Line graphs are used to show a **trend**. A trend is something that happens over time. Look at the line graph below. It shows the number of bluebirds, the state bird of New York, Shakra counted in her yard for five months.

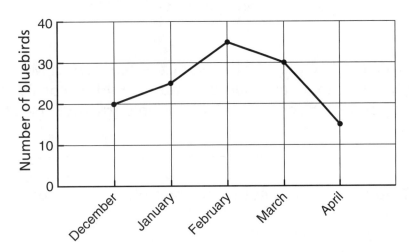

Bluebirds in Shakra's Yard

About how many bluebirds did Shakra see in her yard in December?

_____

During which month did Shakra see the most bluebirds?

_____

If you answered that Shakra saw 20 bluebirds in December and that she saw the most bluebirds in February, you are right. If either of your answers is incorrect, look more carefully at the graph.

A **line plot** is another type of graph. It is used to show how much of a type of data you have. Line plots are great for displaying outliers. An **outlier** is a number that is far away from the rest. Look at the line plot below.

Ages of the Teachers in Manuel's School

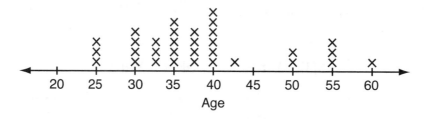

Age

You can see from the line plot that most of the teachers in Manuel's school are between the ages of 30 and 40. What age would be considered an outlier (a data point that doesn't look like it belongs with the others)?

_____

If you said 60, you are right. It lies far to the right of the group of data points.

Practice Questions

Practice 31: Line Graphs

Directions for the Open-Ended Question

The following question is an open-ended question. Remember to:

Read the question carefully and think about the answer.

Answer all the parts of the question.

Show your work or explain your answer.

1. **Look at the line graph below.**

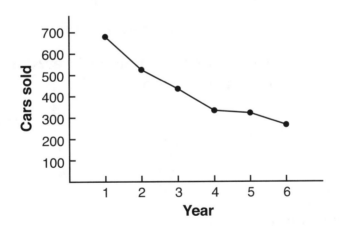

Number of Cars Sold

What can you conclude from the graph about the number of cars sold over the years?

_____

_____

_____

Making Predictions from Data

You can use data to **make a prediction** or **draw a conclusion** about events. When you predict, you guess what will happen in the future. When you draw a conclusion, you decide what the data means.

Every year Monica's grade school class collects newspapers for recycling. Look at the bar graph below.

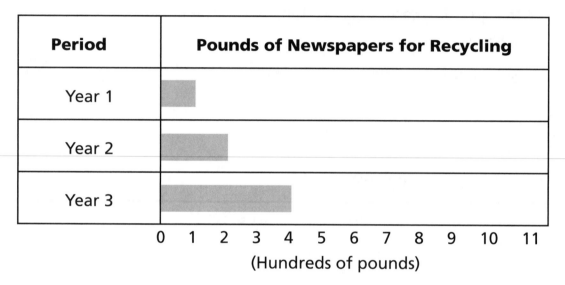

Period	Pounds of Newspapers for Recycling
Year 1	
Year 2	
Year 3	

0 1 2 3 4 5 6 7 8 9 10 11
(Hundreds of pounds)

The Recycling Center pays cash for each pound of newspapers. In which year did Monica's class raise the most money?

Ⓐ   Year 1

Ⓑ   Year 2

Ⓒ   Year 3

Ⓓ   cannot tell from this data

Read the bar graph. You can see that the bar next to Year 3 is the longest. In Year 3, Monica's class collected 400 pounds of newspapers. You can draw the conclusion that the greatest weight of newspapers brought the most money in recycling. Answer choice C is correct.

Let's try one more.

Assume that the trend in the bar graph continues. In which year will Monica's class collect 800 pounds of newspapers?

    Ⓐ Year 4

    Ⓑ Year 5

    Ⓒ Year 6

    Ⓓ cannot tell from this data

Again, look closely at the bar graph. You can make this prediction based on data. Each year, the total is about two times the amount of the year before. If Monica's class doubles their total from Year 3, they would collect 800 pounds in Year 4. Answer choice A is correct.

Practice Questions

Practice 32: Making Predictions from Data

DIRECTIONS:

Choose the best of the answer choices given for each of the following problems. Fill in the circle next to your choice.

1. Joaquin runs a limeade stand in the summer. The graph shows the average number of limeades he sells each day. His mother says he can work at the stand only three days a week now. To make the most money, which day should he drop from his schedule?

Joaquin's Limeade Stand

Thursday	24 cups sold
Friday	15 cups sold
Saturday	32 cups sold
Sunday	38 cups sold

ⓐ Thursday

ⓑ Friday

ⓒ Saturday

ⓓ Sunday

HINT

Should Joaquin drop a day with more sales or less sales on average?

2. **The line graph below shows the changes in Josh's height over five years. If the trend continues, how tall will Josh be in his sixth year?**

Josh's Height Over Five Years

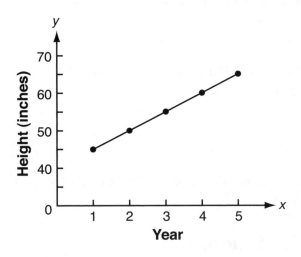

Ⓐ 60 inches

Ⓑ 65 inches

Ⓒ 70 inches

Ⓓ more than 70 inches

To make a prediction from this graph, notice the trend of the graph line. Where will it be on Year 6?

Practice Questions

End-of-Chapter Practice Problems

DIRECTIONS:

Choose the best of the answer choices given for each of the following problems. Fill in the circle next to your choice.

1. The pictograph below shows the number of laps students ran during a special event at school.

Laps Run by Students

Jackie	🏃 🏃 🏃 🏃 🏃
Nicole	🏃 🏃 🏃
Sam	🏃 🏃 🏃 🏃 🏃 🏃
Peter	🏃 🏃 🏃 🏃 🏃

Key: 🏃 = 2 laps

How many laps did Sam run?

Ⓐ 5

Ⓑ 6

Ⓒ 12

Ⓓ 18

HINT

Determine the number of laps by using the key 🏃 = 2 laps.

2. **How much did it snow in Becky's town in Year 3, according to the following bar graph?**

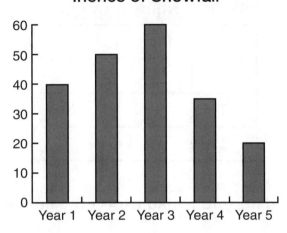

Inches of Snowfall

(A) 40

(B) 50

(C) 60

(D) 70

HINT

Find the bar for Year 3. How high does it go?

3. The table below shows the number of birds at Lee's bird feeder each
    hour during a recent day.

Hour	Number of Birds
1	15
2	13
3	10
4	6

Judging from this data, you would expect the number of birds in Hour 5
to be

Ⓐ less than 6

Ⓑ 6

Ⓒ more than 6

Ⓓ more than 15

> Look for a trend in the data from hour to hour.

4. Here is a line plot of the ages of people at the water park. Which age
    would be an outlier for this set of data?

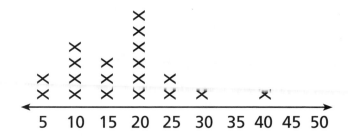

Ⓐ 20

Ⓑ 15

Ⓒ 10

Ⓓ 40

> If you need to, reread the section on line plots in
> this chapter.

New York State Testing Program

MATHEMATICS Grade 4

Practice Test 1

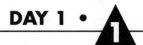

TIPS FOR TAKING THE TEST:

Here are some suggestions to help you do your best:

- Be sure to read carefully all the directions in the test book.

- Read each question carefully and think about the answer before choosing your response.

- On the multiple-choice questions, circle the letter next to the answer you choose.

 This picture means that you will use your ruler.

Session 1

Directions for Students:

This section of the test has 25 multiple-choice questions. You will circle the letter next to the answer you choose. You may NOT use a calculator.

1 During the year, two thousand one hundred thirty-two books were checked out of the school library. What is another way to write this number?

   A   232

   B   2,123

   C   2,132

   D   2,232

2   Use your ruler to help you solve this problem.

The drawing below shows the bookmark Charlene bought.

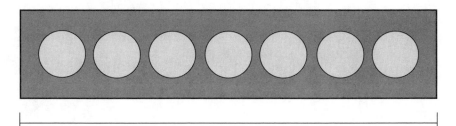

How many centimeters long is Charlene's bookmark?

A   10

B   11

C   12

D   13

3 There were 127 students at Saturday's Health Fair. What is 127 rounded to the nearest ten?

    A   120

    B   125

    C   130

    D   140

4 Hakeem read a 120-page book in 10 days. Hakeem read the same number of pages each day. How many pages did Hakeem read each day?

    A   12

    B   10

    C   9

    D   8

5 Lucy covered a poster board with square stickers, as shown below.

POSTER BOARD

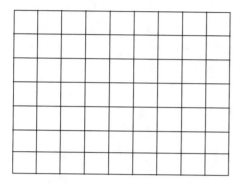

KEY
☐ = 1 square unit

What is the area, in square units, of the poster board?

A   60

B   63

C   70

D   72

6 The Bedford Bugle newspaper has 9,017 readers. What is another way to write this number?

   A   nine hundred seventeen

   B   nine thousand seven

   C   nine thousand seventeen

   D   nine thousand seventy-one

7 Which number when multiplied by any odd number **always** results in an even number?

   A   1

   B   5

   C   7

   D   8

8 Tanya bought 7 packages of candles for her aunt's birthday cake. Each package contained 8 candles. How many candles did Tanya buy in all?

   A   49

   B   54

   C   56

   D   63

9 There are 11 books in the Mystery Hawk series. At Franklin Elementary, 9 students own every book in the series. How many Mystery Hawk books do the students own?

A 99

B 89

C 88

D 79

10 Patrick drew a quadrilateral on the blackboard. The figure had the same number of sides and angles. What is that number?

A 3

B 4

C 5

D 6

11   Lucy wants to check that she correctly solved the number sentence below.

$$15 \times 3 = 45$$

What number sentence should Lucy use to see if her answer is correct?

A $45 \times 15 = \square$

B $15 \div 3 = \square$

C $45 \times 3 = \square$

D $45 \div 3 = \square$

12 This bar graph shows the number of each kind of school supply Ben purchased last week.

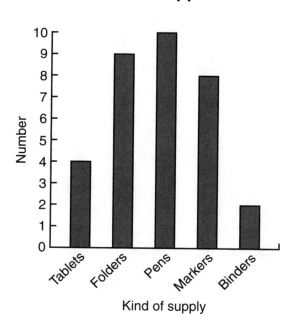

School Supplies

How many pens and markers did Ben purchase?

A　8

B　10

C　18

D　20

13   This week, the Acme Company made 4,621 race car toys. Last week, the company made 3,621 race car toys. What is the difference between 4,621 and 3,621?

    A   ten tens

    B   fifty tens

    C   ten hundreds

    D   ten thousands

14   Keith wrote the number sentence below.

$$245 < \underline{\quad\quad}$$

What number can Keith write on the line to make the number sentence correct?

    A   246

    B   245

    C   244

    D   144

15 Which expression is equal to $17 \times (82 \times 56)$?

   A $(17 \times 82) + 56$

   B $17 \times (82 + 56)$

   C $(17 + 82) \times 56$

   D $(17 \times 82) \times 56$

16 Suki bought a large sack of birdseed at the pet store. Which unit of measure is **best** for measuring how much the sack weighs?

   A   gram

   B   kilogram

   C   liter

   D   milliliter

17 Which input-output table follows the rule below?

Input ÷ 3 = Output

A

Input	Output
16	8
14	7
12	6
10	5

C

Input	Output
18	6
21	7
24	8
27	9

B

Input	Output
9	3
10	4
11	5
12	6

D

Input	Output
6	18
7	21
8	24
9	27

18 Michele's school is visiting the state fair. The Whirl-A-Way ride can carry 22 students at one time. Michele estimates that it will take 15 rides for all 297 students to get one ride. Which expression can be used to check whether Michele's estimation is reasonable?

A $300 \div 20$

B $300 \div 30$

C $400 \div 20$

D $400 \div 25$

19 Devon wants to measure the length of an envelope. Which unit of measure is best for Devon to use?

A   yard

B   centimeter

C   meter

D   kilometer

20 Which list shows the fractions in order from **greatest** to **least**?

   A $\frac{1}{4}$, $\frac{1}{2}$, $\frac{1}{3}$

   B $\frac{1}{4}$, $\frac{1}{3}$, $\frac{1}{2}$

   C $\frac{1}{3}$, $\frac{1}{2}$, $\frac{1}{4}$

   D $\frac{1}{2}$, $\frac{1}{3}$, $\frac{1}{4}$

21 The two statements below describe the number of apples, bananas, and oranges Kwan's family ate for breakfast.

   the number of apples < the number of oranges
   the number of apples > the number of bananas

Which could be the number of apples, bananas, and oranges that Kwan's family ate?

   A   6 apples, 5 bananas, 7 oranges

   B   5 apples, 6 bananas, 7 oranges

   C   7 apples, 6 bananas, 5 oranges

   D   6 apples, 7 bananas, 5 oranges

22   Which pair of figures are congruent?

A
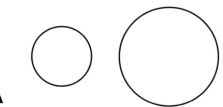

B

C
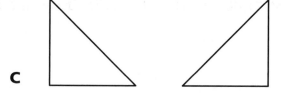

D
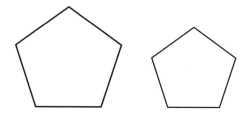

23 Ms. Beatty bought a new carton of eggs. She used 6 of the 12 eggs to make omelets for breakfast. Which fraction is equivalent to 6/12?

A $\frac{1}{4}$

B $\frac{1}{2}$

C $\frac{1}{6}$

D $\frac{1}{3}$

24 Oscar and his grandfather went bird-watching in the woods. They began at 7:30 A.M. and finished at 11:00 A.M. How long did Oscar and his grandfather look for birds?

A 2 hours

B 2 hours 30 minutes

C 3 hours

D 3 hours 30 minutes

25 The Jets baseball team held a cookout. Coach Smith cooked 24 hot dogs for the team. Each of the 9 players ate 2 hot dogs. How many hot dogs were left?

A   5

B   6

C   7

D   8

26 Three students did pull-ups on a bar. Roberto did 5 more pull-ups than Janet. Janet did 3 times as many pull-ups as Viola. Viola did 9 pull-ups. How many pull-ups did Roberto do?

A   27

B   30

C   32

D   36

27 Four students have savings accounts. Every month, the students add the same number of dollars to their savings accounts as the month before. The table below shows the total amount of money each student has at the end of each month.

Savings Accounts

Month	Total Savings (in dollars)			
	Tamara	Bashir	Emily	Brett
1	?	?	?	?
2	62	69	64	67
3	68	72	69	71
4	74	75	74	75

If the students have saved the same number of dollars each month, who had the least money at the end of Month 1?

A Tamara

B Bashir

C Emily

D Brett

28   A diagram of a parking lot is shown below. Part of the parking lot is for cars, and part of the lot is for buses.

PARKING LOT

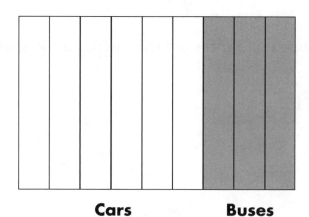

Cars   **Buses**

What fraction of the parking lot is reserved for buses?

A $\frac{1}{2}$

B $\frac{1}{3}$

C $\frac{1}{4}$

D $\frac{1}{8}$

29 Adrian wrote the open sentences below.

If both of Adrian's open sentences are true, which open sentence is also true?

A

B ⬤ < ✦

C ✦ > ⬤

D ✦ > △

30 Jackie's homework included drawing a pentagon. Jackie draws the two line segments shown below when she is interrupted by a phone call.

How many **more** line segments must Jackie draw to complete the pentagon?

A 6

B 5

C 4

D 3

TIPS FOR TAKING THE TEST:

Here are some suggestions to help you do your best:

- Be sure to read carefully all the directions in the test book.

- Read each question carefully and think about the answer before choosing your response.

- Be sure to show your work when asked. You may receive partial credit if you have shown your work.

Session 2

Directions for Students:

This section of the test has short-response and extended-response questions. Show your work in the space provided. You may NOT use a calculator.

31 Last night, 9,387 people attended the circus at Madison Square Garden. Tonight, 7,934 people attended. How many more people were at the circus last night than tonight?

Show your work.

Answer _____ people

32 A factory can make 83 footballs in 1 hour. What is the total number of footballs the factory can make in 7 hours?

Show your work.

Answer _____ footballs

33   Madison buys a leash for her dog. The leash is 4 feet 9 inches long. How long in **inches** is the leash?

Show your work.

Answer _____ inches

34 J.D. has $5.00 to spend on food at the carnival. Prices for items at the carnival are shown below.

> ### Carnival Snack Bar
>
> Hot Dog..$2.25
> Peanuts..$1.45
> Pizza Slice.....................................$3.50
> Fudge Bar.....................................$0.90
> Shake...$3.00

Write three different items that J.D. can buy that total less than $5.00.

_____   _____   _____

If J.D. buys the items, how much money will he have left over?

Show your work

Answer $ _____

35   Akira drew the diagram of his bedroom floor shown below.

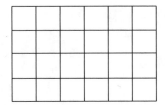

KEY
⊢─┤   = 1 unit
☐   = 1 square unit

Part A

What is the **perimeter**, in units, of Akira's bedroom floor?

Show your work.

Answer _____ units

Part B

What is the **area**, in square units, of the bedroom floor?

Answer _____ square units

36　Dana writes a total of 59 spelling words on 7 blank cards. On each of the first 6 cards, she writes 9 spelling words. How many words does Dana write on the last card?

Show your work.

Answer _____ words

37 Coach Martin has a group of 35 players. He wants to divide them into teams. Each team will have 5 players. He writes the number sentence below to find the number of teams.

$$35 \div 5 = ?$$

How many teams does Coach Martin make from the group of players?

Answer _____ teams

Complete the number sentence below that could be used to check to see that your answer is correct.

Number Sentence _____ = 35

38 Maria saves money for a new telescope. Maria's mom gives her a certain amount of money for each dollar she saves. The table below shows how much money Maria has saved and how much money her mother has given her.

Maria's Telescope Money

Maria	Mother
$4	$16
$5	$20
$6	$24
$7	$28

Part A

If the pattern in the table continues, how much money will Maria's mother have given her when Maria saves $9?

Answer $ _____

Part B

On the lines below, explain the rule to find the number of dollars Maria's mother gives her.

_____

_____

_____

_____

_____

39 Derek, Alisha, and Kaye sold tickets to the school play. The table below shows the number of tickets each student sold over three days.

TICKET SALES FOR SCHOOL PLAY

Student	Number of Tickets		
	Wednesday	**Thursday**	**Friday**
Derek	5	4	2
Alisha	5	9	4
Kaye	2	7	5

Part A

On the lines below, write the total number of tickets each student sold over the three days.

Derek _____ tickets

Alisha _____ tickets

Kaye _____ tickets

Part B

On the grid below, make a bar graph to show the total number of tickets each student sold.

Be sure to:

- title the graph
- label both axes
- provide a scale for the graph
- graph all the data

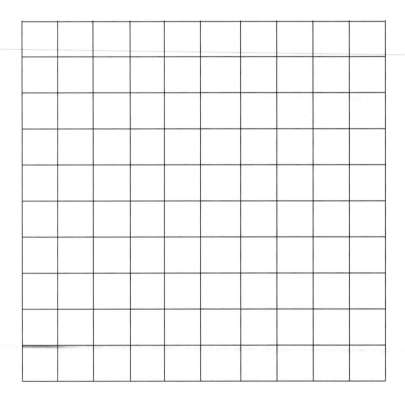

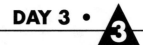
TIPS FOR TAKING THE TEST:

Here are some suggestions to help you do your best:

- Be sure to read carefully all the directions in the test book.

- Read each question carefully and think about the answer before choosing your response.

- Be sure to show your work when asked. You may receive partial credit if you have shown your work.

Session 3

Directions for Students:

This section of the test has short-response and extended-response questions. Show your work in the space provided. You may NOT use a calculator.

40 Kristin is making 13 fruit salads for a picnic. She places 8 strawberries in each fruit salad. What is the total number of strawberries that Kristin uses for her fruit salads?

Show your work.

Answer _____ strawberries

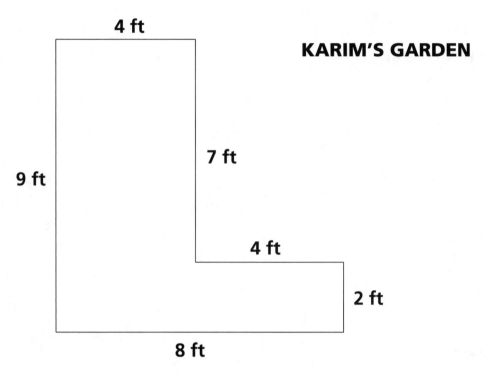
41 Karim is putting a rock border around his vegetable garden, as shown below.

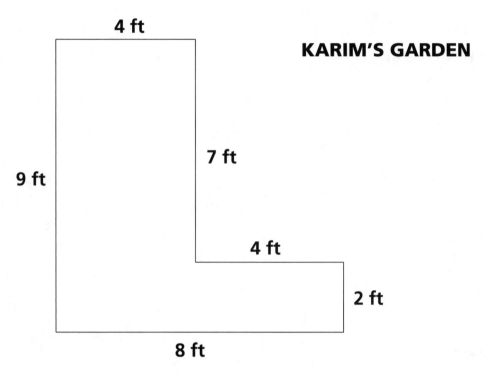

4 ft

KARIM'S GARDEN

7 ft

9 ft

4 ft

2 ft

8 ft

(Not drawn to scale)

What is the perimeter, in feet, of Karim's garden?

Show your work.

Answer _____ feet

42 Andrew bought a notebook for $3.08 and a marker for $0.87. He gave the cashier a ten-dollar bill. How much money did Andrew receive in change?

Show your work.

Answer $ _____

43 Suong is making 45 necklaces with beads. The table below shows the total number of necklaces she has made by the end of weeks 2 through 5.

SUONG'S NECKLACES

Week	Total Number of Necklaces
2	10
3	15
4	20
5	25

Part A

If the pattern in the table continues, how many necklaces will Suong have made by the end of Week 6?

Answer _____ necklaces

On the lines below, explain how you found your answer.

_____

_____

_____

_____

_____

Part B

If the pattern in the table continues, by the end of which week will Suong have made the 45th necklace?

Answer Week _____

44   Mr. Kovacs bought 9 boxes of eggs. There are 12 eggs in each box.

Part A

What is the total number of eggs in the 9 boxes?

Show your work.

Answer _____ eggs

Part B

Write a number sentence that finds the total number of eggs in 5 of the boxes.

Number Sentence _____ = _____

45   Russell writes the number pattern below.

1, 3, 9, 27, ___?___

What is the next number in the pattern?

Answer _____

On the line below, write the rule for Russell's pattern.

Rule _____

46   Manuel has a total of 57 marbles in 3 jars. Each jar has the same number of marbles. How many marbles are in each jar?

Show your work.

Answer _____ marbles

47 The bar graph below shows the low temperatures for Buffalo, New York, for four days in January.

LOW TEMPERATURES IN BUFFALO

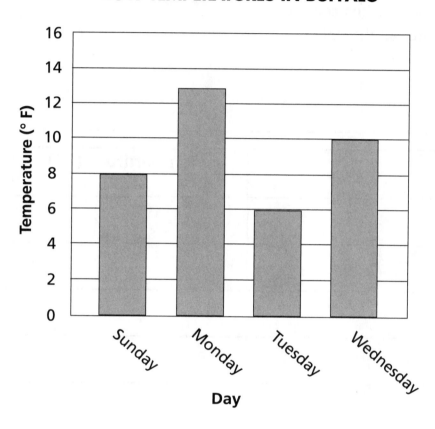

Complete the table below to show the low temperatures in Buffalo during the four days shown in the graph.

Be sure to:

- title the table
- label the first column
- enter all the data

_____

	Temperature (° F)

48

Part A

Each expression in the first column below is equivalent to one of the expressions in the second column. Draw a line between the pairs of expressions that are equivalent. The first line has been drawn for you.

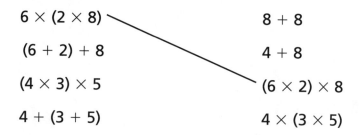

$6 \times (2 \times 8)$ $8 + 8$

$(6 + 2) + 8$ $4 + 8$

$(4 \times 3) \times 5$ $(6 \times 2) \times 8$

$4 + (3 + 5)$ $4 \times (3 \times 5)$

Part B

Greta wrote the number sentence below.

$(5 \times 2) \times 4 = 40$

Oliver rewrote Greta's number sentence and grouped the numbers differently. Complete Oliver's number sentence below to show the new grouping. Use all the numbers and symbols from Greta's number sentence.

Oliver's Number Sentence _____ $= 40$

New York State Testing Program

MATHEMATICS Grade 4

Practice Test 2

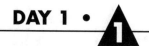

TIPS FOR TAKING THE TEST:

Here are some suggestions to help you do your best:

- Be sure to read carefully all the directions in the test book.

- Read each question carefully and think about the answer before choosing your response.

- On the multiple-choice questions, circle the letter next to the answer you choose.

 This picture means that you will use your ruler.

Session 1

Directions for Students:

This section of the test has 25 multiple-choice questions. You will circle the letter next to the answer you choose. You may NOT use a calculator.

1 At the U.S. Open tennis tournament, nine thousand seven hundred thirty-eight people bought tickets for one session. What is another way to write this number?

A 9,738

B 9,378

C 9,038

D 938

2

Use your ruler to help you solve this problem.

How many centimeters long is the pencil shown below?

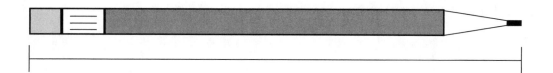

A   11

B   12

C   13

D   14

3   Douglass Elementary has 932 books in its library. What is 932 rounded to the nearest hundred?

   A   800

   B   900

   C   930

   D   1,000

4   Lena shoots 100 free throws every day for practice. How many days does it take Lena to shoot 800 free throws?

   A   7

   B   8

   C   10

   D   12

5 Daniel used a ruler to draw a pattern of squares on a sheet of paper. The squares cover the sheet completely.

SHEET OF PAPER

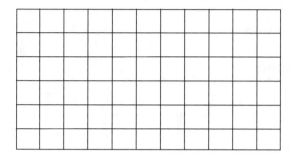

KEY
▢ = 1 square unit

What is the area, in square units, of the sheet of paper?

A 56

B 60

C 63

D 66

6   There are 7,299 people listed in the phone book for Elmwood City. What is another way to write this number?

     A   seven thousand two hundred ninety-nine

     B   seven thousand two hundred ninety

     C   seven thousand twenty-nine

     D   seven hundred ninety-nine

7   Which number when multiplied by **any** odd number always results in an odd number?

     A   2

     B   4

     C   5

     D   8

8   Raymond buys 9 packages of hot dog buns for a cookout. Each package contains 8 buns. How many hot dog buns does Raymond buy in all?

     A   16

     B   63

     C   72

     D   81

9   There are 12 tables in the YMCA snack bar. Each table has 7 chairs around it. How many chairs are there in the snack bar?

A   70

B   72

C   81

D   84

10   Tamara wrote the riddle below.

I have 8 sides.
I have 8 angles.
What am I?

What shape does the riddle describe?

A   hexagon

B   octagon

C   quadrilateral

D   pentagon

GO ON

11　Jessica wants to check her answer to the number sentence below.

$$36 \div 3 = 12$$

Which number sentence could Jessica use to see if her answer is correct?

A　$3 \times 12 = \square$

B　$12 \div 3 = \square$

C　$36 \times 12 = \square$

D　$36 \times 3 = \square$

12 The number of vehicles in a parking lot are shown below.

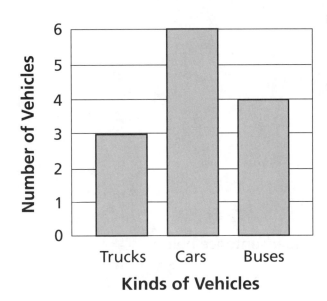

VEHICLES IN A PARKING LOT

Based on the information in the bar graph, which statement is true?

A More than half of all the vehicles are cars.

B The number of cars is two times the number of trucks.

C The number of cars is two times the number of buses.

D Exactly half of all the vehicles are cars.

13 In a video game, Ronald earned a score of 36,428 points. His friend Gina earned a score of 46,428 points on the same game. What is the difference between 36,428 and 46,428?

  A 10 tens

  B 10 hundreds

  C 50 hundreds

  D 10 thousands

14 Grace wrote the number sentence below.

$$\_\_\_\_\_ > 125$$

Which number can Grace write on the line to make the number sentence correct?

  A 106

  B 124

  C 125

  D 126

15 Which expression is equal to (21 × 53) × 36?

A   (21 + 53) + 36

B   (21 × 53) + 36

C   21 × (53 × 36)

D   21 × (53 + 36)

16 Lacey wants to measure the length of the classroom. Which unit of measure is best for Lacey to use?

A   centimeter

B   inch

C   meter

D   kilometer

17   Which input-output table follows the rule below?

Input × 2 = Output

A

Input	Output
20	10
16	8
14	7
12	6

C

Input	Output
23	25
26	28
29	31
31	33

B

Input	Output
4	12
6	18
8	24
10	30

D

Input	Output
1	2
3	6
5	10
7	14

18   Each school bus at Roosevelt Elementary can carry 42 students. There are 392 students going on the school field trip. Miguel estimates that 10 buses are needed for the trip. Which expression can be used to check whether Miguel's estimation is reasonable?

A $400 \div 30$

B $400 \div 40$

C $300 \div 30$

D $300 \div 40$

19   The teacher's lounge has packets of sugar for coffee or tea. Which unit of measure is **best** for measuring how much each packet of sugar weighs?

A   gram

B   kilogram

C   liter

D   milliliter

20 Which list shows the fractions in order from **least** to **greatest**?

A $\frac{1}{4}, \frac{1}{3}, \frac{1}{2}$

B $\frac{1}{2}, \frac{1}{4}, \frac{1}{3}$

C $\frac{1}{4}, \frac{1}{2}, \frac{1}{3}$

D $\frac{1}{3}, \frac{1}{2}, \frac{1}{4}$

21 The two statements below describe the number of dogs, cats, and hamsters living in Jason's house.

the number of hamsters > the number of dogs
the number of cats < the number of dogs

Which could be the number of dogs, cats, and hamsters living in Jason's house?

A   5 dogs, 3 cats, 4 hamsters

B   4 dogs, 3 cats, 5 hamsters

C   3 dogs, 4 cats, 5 hamsters

D   4 dogs, 5 cats, 3 hamsters

22 Which pair of figures are similar?

A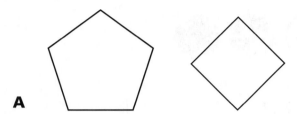

B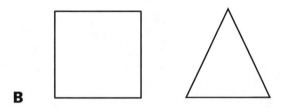

C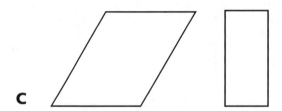

D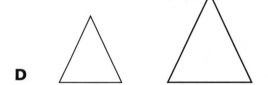

23 Dustin drew the circles below. Two of the 6 circles are black.

Which fraction is equivalent to 2/6?

A $\frac{1}{3}$

B $\frac{1}{4}$

C $\frac{1}{2}$

D $\frac{2}{3}$

24 Jorge and Ben started to clean the garage at 1:30 P.M. They finished at 4:00 P.M. How long did it take them to complete the job?

A   1 hour 30 minutes

B   2 hours

C   2 hours 30 minutes

D   3 hours

25 Paula opens a 22-ounce jar of salsa. She pours 3 ounces of salsa on each of 5 enchiladas. How many ounces of salsa are left in the jar?

A 5

B 7

C 8

D 10

26 Claire can do 3 times as many sit-ups as Tim. Tim can do 5 more sit-ups than Whitney. Whitney can do 15 sit-ups. How many sit-ups can Claire do?

A 60

B 62

C 65

D 70

27 Four students have savings accounts. Every month, the students add the same number of dollars to their savings accounts as the month before. The table below shows the total amount of money each student has at the end of each month.

Students' Savings Accounts

Month	Total Savings (in dollars)			
	Henry	Olivia	Mina	Tony
1	35	33	36	38
2	40	39	40	41
3	45	45	44	44

If the students continue to save the same number of dollars each month, who will have the **most** money at the end of month 5?

A   Henry

B   Olivia

C   Mina

D   Tony

28 A diagram of a park is shown below. Part of the park is covered with grass, and part of the park is covered with sand.

Murray Park

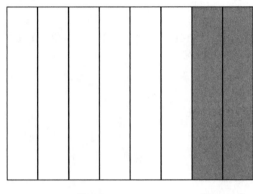

Grass   **Sand**

What fraction of the park is covered with sand?

A $\frac{1}{8}$

B $\frac{1}{3}$

C $\frac{1}{2}$

D $\frac{1}{4}$

29 DeJuan wrote the open sentences below.

If both of DeJuan's open sentences are true, which open sentence is also true?

A

B ◯ > ✦

C △ > ✦

D △ < ✦

30 Mark started to draw a hexagon. He drew the 2 line segments shown below before his pencil broke.

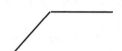

How many **more** line segments must Mark draw to complete the hexagon?

A 3

B 4

C 5

D 6

STOP

TIPS FOR TAKING THE TEST:

Here are some suggestions to help you do your best:

- Be sure to read carefully all the directions in the test book.

- Read each question carefully and think about the answer before choosing your response.

- Be sure to show your work when asked. You may receive partial credit if you have shown your work.

Session 2

Directions for Students:

This section of the test has short-response and extended-response questions. Show your work in the space provided. You may NOT use a calculator.

31 Last month, 3,988 people visited the city museum. This month, 5,012 people visited the museum. How many more people visited the museum this month than visited last month?

Show your work.

Answer _____ people

32 A factory can make 57 trucks in 1 day. What is the total number of trucks the factory can make in 8 days?

Show your work.

Answer _____ trucks

33 Mr. London buys a board at the lumber yard. The board is 5 feet 8 inches long. How long, in **inches**, is the board?

Show your work.

Answer _____ inches

34 Jolene has $10.00 to spend on food at the football game. Prices for food items at the stadium snack bar are shown below.

Stadium Snack Bar

Pizza Slice $4.75
Hot Dog $3.25
Cheese Nachos $3.50
Chicken Sandwich $6.25
Lemonade $2.50

Write three different items that Jolene can buy that total less than $10.00.

_____   _____   _____

If Jolene buys the three items, what amount of money will she have left over?

Show your work

Answer $ _____

35 Fernando drew the diagram of the garage floor shown below.

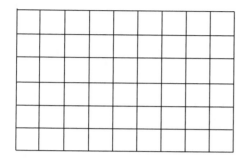

KEY	
⊢—┤	= 1 unit
☐	= 1 square unit

Part A

What is the **perimeter**, in units, of Fernando's garage floor?

Show your work.

Answer _____ units

Part B

What is the **area**, in square units, of the garage floor?

Answer _____ square units

36 Andrew writes a total of 44 names on 7 blank cards. On each of the first 6 cards he writes 7 names. How many names does Andrew write on the last card?

Show your work.

Answer _____ names

37 Ms. Sulu plants a group of 56 flowers in 7 large pots. She plants the exact same number of flowers in each pot. She writes the number sentence below to find the number of flowers for each pot.

$$56 \div 7 = ?$$

How many flowers does Ms. Sulu plant in each pot?

Answer _____ flowers

Complete the number sentence below that could be used to check to see that your answer is correct.

Number Sentence _____ = 56

38 Walter saves money for a camera. Walter's dad gives him a certain amount of money for each dollar he saves. The table below shows how much money Walter has saved and how much money his father has given him.

WALTER'S CAMERA MONEY

Walter	Dad
$3	$9
$4	$12
$5	$15
$6	$18

Part A

If the pattern in the table continues, how much money will Walter's father have given him when Walter saves $10?

Answer $ _____

Part B

On the lines below, explain the rule to find the number of dollars Walter's dad gives him.

_____

_____

_____

_____

_____

39 Lucinda, Alex, and Marta held a contest to read the most books in the summer. The table below shows the number of books each student read over 3 months.

BOOKS READ IN THE CONTEST

Student	Number of Books		
	June	July	August
Lucinda	5	3	6
Alex	4	5	7
Marta	7	4	8

Part A

On the lines below, write the total number of books each student read over the three months.

Lucinda _____ books

Alex _____ books

Marta _____ books

Part B

On the grid below, make a bar graph to show the total number of books each student read.

Be sure to:

- title the graph
- label both axes
- provide a scale for the graph
- graph all the data

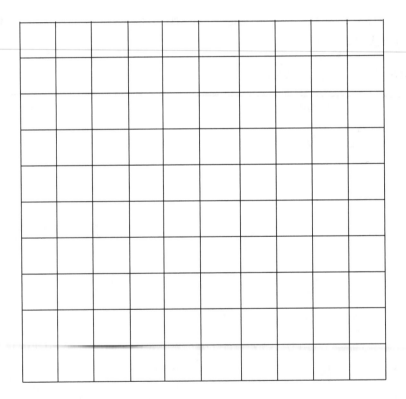

TIPS FOR TAKING THE TEST:

Here are some suggestions to help you do your best:

- Be sure to read carefully all the directions in the test book.

- Read each question carefully and think about the answer before choosing your response.

- Be sure to show your work when asked. You may receive partial credit if you have shown your work.

Session 3

Directions for Students:

This section of the test has short-response and extended-response questions. Show your work in the space provided. You may NOT use a calculator.

40   Trudy has a total of 72 puppets in 6 boxes. Each box has the same number of puppets. How many puppets are in each box?

Show your work.

Answer _____ puppets

41 Ms. Landon is putting a brick border around her patio, as shown below.

Ms. Landon's Patio

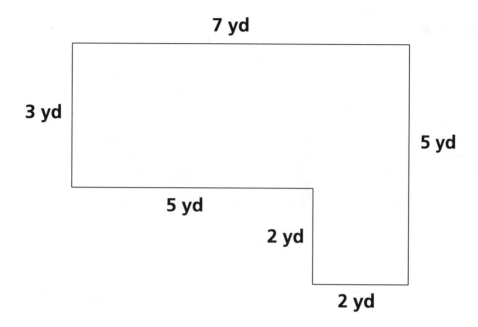

7 yd

3 yd

5 yd

5 yd

2 yd

2 yd

What is the perimeter, in yards, of Ms. Landon's patio?

Show your work.

Answer _____ yards

42　Amber bought a sketchbook for $3.82 and a pencil for $0.39. She gave the cashier $5.00. How much money did Amber receive in change?

Show your work.

Answer $ _____

43 Mr. Sanchez is making 75 fancy belt buckles. The table below shows the total number of buckles he has made by the end of weeks 3 through 6.

MR. SANCHEZ'S BELT BUCKLES

Week	Total Number of Necklaces
3	21
4	28
5	35
6	42

Part A

If the pattern in the table continues, how many belt buckles will Mr. Sanchez have made by the end of Week 8?

Answer _____ buckles

On the lines below, explain how you found your answer.

_____

_____

_____

_____

Part B

If the pattern in the table continues, by the end of which week will Mr. Sanchez have made the 75th belt buckle?

Answer Week _____

44   Sandy bought 11 boxes of pens. There are 7 pens in each box.

Part A

What is the total number of pens in the 11 boxes?

Show your work.

Answer _____ pens

Part B

Write a number sentence that finds the total number of pens in 4 of the boxes.

Number Sentence _____ = _____

45   Lars writes the number pattern below.

45, 42, 39, 36, _____?_____

What is the next number in the pattern?

Answer _____

On the line below, write the rule for Lars' pattern.

Rule _____

46   Tamara is making 15 bracelets with beads. She puts 6 blue beads on each bracelet. What is the total number of blue beads that Tamara uses for her bracelets?

Show your work.

Answer _____ blue beads

GO ON

47 The bar graph below shows the number of home runs hit by the New York Yankees in four months of the baseball season.

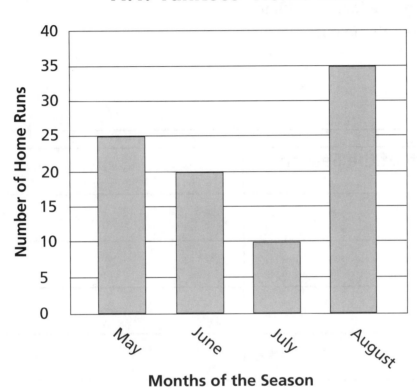

Complete the table below to show the home runs hit by the Yankees team during the four months shown in the graph.

Be sure to:

- title the table
- label the second column
- enter all the data

_____

Month of the Season	

48

Part A

Each expression in the first column below is equivalent to one of the expressions in the second column. Draw a line between the pairs of expressions that are equivalent. The first line has been drawn for you.

7 + (3 + 2)	8 + 5
6 × (3 × 2)	8 × (2 × 4)
(8 × 2) × 4	(6 × 3) × 2
(6 + 2) + 5	7 + 5

Part B

Cam wrote the number sentence below.

$$9 \times (2 \times 1) = 18$$

Dwight rewrote Cam's number sentence and grouped the numbers differently. Complete Dwight's number sentence below to show the new grouping. Use all the numbers and symbols from Cam's number sentence.

Dwight's Number Sentence _____ = 18

STOP

Answer Key
Chapter 1 Answer Explanations

Practice 1: Whole Numbers and Place Value

1. C

This number is three hundred and fifty thousand. The 5 is in the ten thousands place.

2. A

The 4 in the number 8,274,527 stands for 4 thousands.

3. B

The number is written as 4,844.

4. C

Answer choice C is larger than A and B in the hundreds place and larger than choice D in the tens place.

Practice 2: Fractions

1. B

By carefully looking at the shaded areas, you can see that $\frac{5}{12}$ is larger than $\frac{3}{16}$. Choose the > symbol for "greater than."

2. D

$\frac{1}{4}$ is the smallest of the three fractions and $\frac{1}{2}$ is the largest.

3. A

Three-ninths is equivalent to one-third.

Practice 3: Decimals and Money

1. B

A decimal is always smaller than a mixed decimal (which has a decimal and a whole number). So, .34 is definitely the smallest number and should come first. The next two numbers in answer choice B are 1.0 and 1.24. Zero is smaller than 24, so 1.0 is smaller than 1.24.

2. D

The decimal should come first, then the mixed number 1.23, and then 1.50. For the mixed decimals in these answer choices, the whole number parts are equal, so compare the decimal parts.

3. D

The fraction $\frac{3}{4}$ is written as 0.75. So the correct answer is the mixed decimal 3.75.

4. A

8 dollars is 8.00 and 77 cents is 0.77. The correct answer is $8.77.

End-of-Chapter Practice Problems

1. B

Remember that the decimal is the smallest. Since both mixed numbers include the whole number 2, choose the one with the smaller decimal after it for the next number.

2. B

If you look closely at the shaded areas, you'll see that $\frac{5}{9}$ is greater than $\frac{3}{8}$.

3. C

The 1 in the number 9,125,000 has a place value of one hundred thousand.

4. B

The decimal equivalent of $2\frac{1}{4}$ is 2.25.

5. A

Since all the fractions have the same numerator, compare denominators. The fraction $\frac{1}{5}$ has the largest denominator and is the smallest fraction.

6. B

The 4 in the number 6,234,000 has a place value of 4 thousands.

7. D

Six dollars and 32 cents is $6.32 in decimal notation.

8. B

Two of the six beads are blue. This is the same as the fraction $\frac{1}{3}$.

Chapter 2 Answer Explanations

Practice 4: Adding and Subtracting Whole Numbers

1. D

When you correctly add up the numbers, you get 872. Remember to carry the 1 in your addition.

2. C

When you subtract 340 from 8,295, you get 7,955. Remember to borrow in your subtraction.

3. A

When you add 2,131 and 679, you get 2,810.

4. **D**

    To solve this problem correctly, add 125 and 98. The correct answer choice is D, 223.

5. Open-ended question

    $210 + 30 = 240$

    $240 - 53 = 187$

    To solve this problem, you need to first add 210 and 30, and then subtract 53 from this number. The answer is 187 stamps.

Practice 5: Operations with Fractions and Decimals

1. **B**

    Subtract the numerators. The answer is $\frac{4}{12}$.

2. **A**

    $4.45 - 0.45 = 4$.

3. Open-ended question

    $\$0.50 + \$1.25 = \$1.75$

    $\$3.00 - \$1.75 = \$1.25$

    To solve this problem, you need to first add $0.50 and $1.25. Then subtract the sum from $3.00. The answer is $1.25.

Practice 6: Multiplying and Dividing Numbers

1. **C**

    When you divide 2 into 360, the answer is 180.

2. **D**

    When you set up the problem correctly and multiply 38×24, you get 912.

3. Open-ended question

$$8\overline{)172} = 21 \text{ stickers}$$

with work shown:
$$
\begin{array}{r}
21 \\
8\overline{)172} \\
-16 \\
\hline
12 \\
8 \\
\hline
4
\end{array}
$$

21 stickers for each friend
4 stickers left over

Practice 7: Multiplication Rules

1. **A**

    Any number multiplied by 0 is 0.

2. **C**

    This question asks about the associative property. If you multiply three numbers, you can move the parentheses and still get the same answer.

3. **B**

    Any number multiplied by 1 is that number.

4. **C**

    This question asks about the commutative property of multiplication. You can multiply numbers in any order and get the same answer.

End-of-Chapter Practice Problems

1. **B**

    If you add 2,517 and 3,893, you get 6,410.

2. **C**

    The only given number that 12 divides into evenly is 36.

3. **A**

The number 2 divides evenly into 2,420, giving you 1,210.

4. **D**

$148 - 73 = 75$.

5. **C**

Remember to carry the 6. Your result should be 1,273.

6. **B**

Be sure to carry the 1. Your result should be 5.37.

7. **B**

Four apples at $0.35 each equals $1.40. The change from $2.00 is $0.60.

8. **A**

Any number multiplied by 0 is 0.

9. Open-ended question

Divide 8 into 98. The answer is 12 with a remainder of 2.

Mrs. Akiro will have 12 beads on each bracelet, with 2 beads left over.

Chapter 3 Answer Explanations

Practice 8: Estimating Addition

1. **C**

The number 680 rounded to the nearest hundred is 700. The number 292 rounded to the nearest hundred is 300. If you add 700 + 300, you get 1,000. This number is between the 900 and 1,100 range in answer choice C.

2. B

The number 109 rounded to the nearest hundred is 100. The number 258 rounded to the nearest hundred is 300. If you add 100 + 300, you get 400. This number is between 300 and 600, the range in answer choice B.

Practice 9: Estimating Subtraction

1. C

When you round 780 to the nearest hundred, you get 800. When you round 349 to the nearest hundred, you get 300. When you subtract these numbers, the answer is 500. Answer choice C is correct.

2. D

When you round 836 to the nearest hundred, you get 800. When you round 432 to the nearest hundred, you get 400. If you subtract 400 from 800, you get 400. That is between 200 and 500.

Practice 10: Estimating Multiplication

1. C

If you round 43 to 40 and 18 to 20 and multiply, you get 800, so the range 300 to 800 is the correct answer choice, C.

2. C

If you round 29 to 30 and 11 to 10 and multiply, you get 300. Answer choice C is correct.

Practice 11: Estimating Division

1. C

If you round 148 to 100 and divide by 4, you get 25. Answer choice C is correct.

2.   A

If you round 246 to 200 and divide by 6, you get a number close to 33. Another way to do this problem is to round 6 to 5. The number 200 divided by 5 is 40. Answer choice A is correct. If you recognize by mental math that 6 divides evenly into 246, giving an actual quotient of 41, you also get answer choice A.

End-of-Chapter Practice Problems

1.   C

If you round 795 to 800 and 116 to 100 and add 800 and 100, you get 900.

2.   D

If you round 85 to 90 and 12 to 10, you get 900. You could also round 85 to 100 and multiply by 12 to get 1,200. Both answers are in the range in answer choice D.

3.   B

If you round 252 to 300 and divide by 2, you get 150.

4.   C

If you round 925 to 900 and 347 to 300 and subtract 300 from 900, you get 600.

5.   B

If you round 372 to 400 and 108 to 100 and add them, you get 500.

6.   D

If you round 87 to 90 and 12 to 10 and multiply them, you get 900.

7.   B

If you round 114 to 100 and 6 to 10 and divide them, you get 10. (You may be able to divide 100 by 6 directly by mental math to get the range. You don't need an exact answer.)

Chapter 4 Answer Explanations

Practice 12: Lines

1. C

A ray has one endpoint and one arrow.

2. C

The points at the end of a line segment are called endpoints.

3. B

Two lines going in exactly the same direction are called parallel lines.

Practice 13: Angles

1. B

An acute angle is smaller than a right angle. It is less than 90°.

2. A

The other answer choices are either larger or smaller than a right angle.

Practice 14: Two-Dimensional Shapes

1. B

An octagon is any eight-sided figure. The sides don't have to be equal.

2. C

This riddle describes a rectangle.

3. D

The only figure in the answer choices that has four sides is a square.

Practice 15: Three-Dimensional Shapes

1. B

A sphere looks like a ball. It does not have faces or vertices.

2. C

A square pyramid meets this description.

Practice 16: Congruent Shapes

1. A

The rectangles in answer choice A are exactly the same size and shape, so they are congruent.

2. C

These rectangles are different sizes and shapes, so they are **not** congruent.

Practice 17: Perimeter and Area

1. C

When you add up all of the unit edges on the sides of the rectangle, you get $7 + 7 + 4 + 4 = 22$.

2. D

$7 \times 4 = 28$ square units.

3. D

If you add $10 + 10$, you get 20 for the two lengths. When you subtract 20 from 36, the total length of fencing, you get 16. Sixteen divided by 2 is 8, the width of the deck.

End-of-Chapter Practice Problems

1. D

Answer choice D has an obtuse angle, which is greater than 90°.

2. B

There are two lengths and two widths, so multiply 10 by 2 and 4 by 2 and add these numbers. The correct answer is 28.

3. C

A rectangular prism has 6 faces and 8 vertices and looks like a box.

4. D

An obtuse angle measures greater than 90°.

5. D

If you subtract 20, which is twice the width of the room, from 64, you get 44. When you divide this number by 2, you get 22.

6. A

Lines that go in the same direction and don't intersect are parallel lines.

7. B

The point where two rays meet is called the vertex.

8. C

A hexagon is a two-dimensional figure with six sides.

9. Open-ended question

Sample answer: The figure on the left is a cone, and the figure on the right is a cylinder.

A cone has one face, and a cylinder has two.

They are the same in that the faces are circles. They are different in that a cone has a vertex and a cylinder doesn't.

Chapter 5 Answer Explanations

Practice 18: Length

1. **B**

   It might seem like a pretty long way from your bedroom floor to the ceiling, but try to remember the size of each unit of measurement. Inches are too small to use. Miles are used for long distances. Yards would make your bedroom ceiling about three stories high! The best answer choice would be in feet.

2. **A**

   Think of how small a penny is. It's pretty small. Right away you should be able to see that meters, decimeters, and kilometers are far too big to measure such a small object. The correct choice is in centimeters.

Practice 19: Weight

1. **A**

   A car is very heavy, so answer choice A, in tons, is the best answer.

2. **B**

   One gram is a very light weight, and a piece of lettuce is very light.

Practice 20: Capacity

1. **A**

   Two cups of liquid is equal to one pint.

2. **D**

   A swimming pool holds a lot of water. If you measured the amount of water in a pool in cups, it would be a very high number. Pints and quarts are also a little too small to use. The best answer is gallons.

Practice 21: Measuring Time by Hours and Minutes

1.   D

If you add 1 hour and 15 minutes to 2:30, you get 3:45.

2.   C

If you add 30 minutes to 9:10, you get 9:40.

Practice 22: Measuring Time by Days and Weeks

1.   C

April 9 falls on a Friday.

2.   B

There are 4 Saturdays in the month of April shown on the calendar.

End-of-Chapter Practice Problems

1.   D

The most reasonable estimate for the weight of a truck would be in tons. Ounces and pounds are too small.

2.   C

A sidewalk would be measured in meters.

3.   C

If you add 1 hour and 30 minutes to 9:30, you get 11:00.

4.   A

A milliliter is a very small amount of liquid.

5.   B

January 17 falls on a Saturday, so that is the date Gaylene should choose.

Chapter 6 Answer Explanations

Practice 23: Patterns

1.   **C**

The rule assigned to these numbers is to add 8. For example, 6 + 8 = 14, and 14 + 8 = 22.

2.   **B**

Each number decreases by 3. For example, 52 − 3 = 49.

3.   **D**

The complete pattern is square, triangle, circle, triangle.

Practice 24: Functions

1.   **B**

Each number is increased by 9. If you add 9 to 12, the answer is 21.

2.   **B**

Each number is decreased by 3. If you subtract 3 from 9, the answer is 6.

3.   **C**

In the first table, each number is increased by 5. The number 7 in the input row becomes 12 in the output row.

4.   **D**

In the second table, each number is increased by 3. The output from the first machine becomes the input for the second machine. If you add 3 to 12, you get 15.

Practice 25: Input/Output Tables and T-Charts

1. D

Each number is increased by 6. If you add 6 to 12, you get 18.

2. C

The numbers in the *x* column are multiplied by 2 to get the numbers in the *y* column. When the numbers increase but not by the same amount, as here, you should think of multiplication.

Practice 26: Other Kinds of Patterns

1. A

If you repeat the pattern three times, on Day 15 Tammy's grandmother would make fish. On Day 16, the pattern would begin again, and she would make meatloaf.

2. Open-ended

Sample answer: The pattern is that you add $3.25 each week. If you add $3.25 to $15.25, you get $18.50. You would have to save just one more week to have enough money to buy the clock radio. At the end of Week 6, you would have $21.75.

Practice 27: Open Sentences

1. B

By reversing the open sentence, you get $96 \div 12 = \square$, and you can determine that the missing number is 8.

2. D

By reversing the open sentence, you get $72 - 38 = \square$, and you can determine that the missing number is 34.

3.   C

This is a multiplication problem, so you cannot use reversal. Think—what number times 50 gives 150? You should be able to answer this by using mental math.

4.   C

This is the same as $144 \div 12 = \square$, so the missing number is 12.

Practice 28: Equations and Inequalities

1.   D

Since $173 = 173$, choice D is correct.

2.   A

The number 846 is less than 847.

3.   C

Since the circle is greater than the triangle, and the triangle is greater than the hexagon, then the circle must also be greater than the hexagon. Choice C is the correct answer.

Practice 29: Number Sentences

1.   B

If you know that Peter had 24 crayons and now has 36, you can subtract the two numbers to find out how many crayons his mother gave him.

2.   C

This problem also requires subtraction. You need to subtract 24 from 68.

End-of-Chapter Practice Problems

1.   D

The numbers are decreased by 10. If you subtract 10 from 28, the answer is 18.

2.   C

The numbers are increased by 9. For example, $5 + 9 = 14$.

3.   C

Reverse to get $36 \div 3 = \square$, and you can see that the missing number is 12.

4.   B

The numbers are decreased by 6. For example, $18 - 12 = 6$.

5.   D

The only answer choice that 54 is greater than is D, 53.

6.   A

The first number sentence is the correct answer. You need to multiply the number of students, 24, by 2, the number of juice boxes each student will receive.

7.   A

The complete pattern is square, triangle, circle, circle. The next two shapes after the square are a triangle and a circle.

Chapter 7 Answer Explanations

Practice 30: Using Data and Graphs

1. **C**

   Look for football on the bottom of the bar graph. The bar above football goes up to 40.

2. **C**

   The highest bar is soccer. More than 80 students play soccer.

3. **A**

   There are 4 book symbols in Kwan's row. Kwan read 12 books, which is the most of the four students.

Practice 31: Line Graphs

1. Open-ended

   Sample answer: The number of cars sold decreased over the years.

Practice 32: Making Predictions from Data

1. **B**

   On average, Joaquin sells only 15 cups of limeade daily on Fridays. That is the least amount of the 4 days. Joaquin should drop Friday from his schedule.

2. **C**

   The line graph shows that Josh's height will be more than 70 inches by his sixth year. C is the correct answer.

End-of-Chapter Practice Problems

1. **C**

    To solve this problem, you need to look at how many runners are after Sam's name. There are 6. Then you have to multiply this number by 2, which gives you 12.

2. **C**

    The bar for Year 3 goes up to the number 60.

3. **A**

    The number of birds each hour is going down. From the trend, you would expect the number in Hour 5 to be less than 6. Answer A is correct.

4. **D**

    An outlier is a data point that doesn't look like it belongs with the others. The age 40 is the outlier in this set.

Practice Test 1 Answer Explanations

1. **C**   (Number Sense and Operations: 4.N02)

    "Two thousand one hundred thirty-two" is the same as the number 2,132. Answer choice C is correct.

    Answer choice A is incorrect because it is "two hundred thirty-two." Answer choice B is incorrect because it is "two thousand one hundred twenty-three." Answer choice D is incorrect because it is "two thousand two hundred thirty-two."

2.   **B**   (Measurement: 4.M02)

If you use the centimeters part of your ruler, you'll see that the bookmark is 11 centimeters long.

Answer choices A, C, and D are incorrect because they are the wrong measurements for the bookmark.

3.   **C**   (Number Sense and Operations: 4.N26)

The number 127 ends in the digit 7. This is greater than 5, so round it up to the nearest ten. The correct answer is 130.

Answer choice A is incorrect because it was rounded down from 127 to 120. Answer choice B is incorrect because it is not rounded to the nearest ten. Answer choice D is incorrect because it is 10 greater than the nearest ten.

4.   **A**   (Number Sense and Operations: 4.N20)

120 is a multiple of 10. 120 divided by 10 = 12. Answer choice A is correct.

Answer choices B, C, and D are all incorrect due to faulty division.

5.   **B**   (Geometry: 4. G04)

The poster board is divided into 7 rows, with 9 squares in each row. To get the area, multiply 7 x 9, which is 63. Answer choice B is correct.

Answer choices A, C, and D are incorrect because of miscounting the squares or faulty multiplication.

6.   **C**   (Number Sense and Operations: 4.N02)

The correct words for the number 9,017 are "nine thousand seventeen." Answer choice C is correct.

Answer choice A is the same as 917. Answer choice B is the same as 9,007. Answer choice D is the same as 9,071.

7. D   (Number Sense and Operations: 4.N13)

An even number multiplied by an odd number always results in an even number. The only even number among the answers is 8. Answer choice D is correct.

Answer choices A, B, and C are all incorrect because they are odd numbers.

8. C   (Number Sense and Operations: 3.N19)

Seven packages of 8 candles is 7 x 8, or 56. Answer choice C is correct.

Answer choices A, B, and D are incorrect products of 7 and 8.

9. A   (Number Sense and Operations: 3.N20)

9 complete sets with 11 books in each set = 9 x 11 = 99. Answer choice A is correct.

Answer choices B, C, and D are all incorrect. Each would result in a different product than 9 x 11.

10. B   (Geometry: 4.G01)

A quadrilateral is a polygon with 4 sides and 4 angles. The word part *quad-* means "four." Answer choice B is correct.

Answer choice A is incorrect because it is the number for a triangle. Answer choice C is incorrect because it is the number for a pentagon. Answer choice D is incorrect because it is the number for a hexagon.

11. D   (Number Sense and Operations: 4.N17)

Use the inverse operation to check if an answer is correct. The inverse operation of multiplication is division. One way to check if this number sentence is correct is to divide 45 by 3. Answer choice D is correct.

Answer choices A and C are incorrect because they do not use the inverse operation and use the wrong numbers. Answer choice B is incorrect because it divides the wrong numbers to check the correct answer.

12. C   (Statistics and Probability: 4.S06)

Find the bar for pens and the bar for markers. Ben bought 10 pens and 8 markers for a total of 18.

Answer choice A is incorrect because it is the number of markers only. Answer choice B is incorrect because it is the number of pens only. Answer choice D is incorrect because of faulty addition.

13. C   (Number Sense and Operations: 4.N04)

$4,621 - 3,621 = 1,000$, which is 10 hundreds. Answer choice C is correct.

Answer choice A is incorrect because it is 100. Answer choice B is incorrect because it is 500. Answer choice D is incorrect because it is 10,000.

14. A   (Algebra: 3.A01)

The symbol < means "less than." The number 245 is less than 246. Answer choice A is correct.

Answer choice B is incorrect because $245 = 245$. Answer choice C is incorrect because 245 is greater than 244. Answer choice D is incorrect because 245 is greater than 144.

15. D   (Number Sense and Operations: 4.N06)

The associative property of multiplication says that: $(a \times b) \times c = a \times (b \times c)$. Thus: $(17 \times 82) \times 56 = 17 \times (82 \times 56)$. Answer choice D is correct.

Answer choice A is incorrect because the numbers are added together, not multiplied. Answer choice B is incorrect because 82 and 56 are added together, not multiplied. Answer choice C is incorrect because 17 and 82 are added together, not multiplied.

16. B (Measurement: 4.M04)

A large sack of birdseed would be measured in kilograms. Answer choice B is correct.

Answer choice A is incorrect because a gram is too small a unit of measure. Answer choices C and D are incorrect because they are used to measure liquids.

17. C (Algebra: 4.A05)

Answer choice C is correct.

$$18 \div 3 = 6$$
$$21 \div 3 = 7$$
$$24 \div 3 = 8$$
$$27 \div 3 = 9$$

Answer choice A is incorrect because the rule for the box is input $\div$ 2 = output. Answer choice B is incorrect because the rule for the box is input − 6 = output. Answer choice D is incorrect because the rule for it is input $\times$ 3 = output.

18. A (Number Sense and Operations: 4.N27)

The estimate would be the total number of students (297) divided by the number of students on each ride (22). 297 can be rounded to 300. 22 can be rounded to 20. 300 divided by 20 is correct.

Answer choices B, C, and D use incorrect rounding to make the estimate.

19. B (Measurement: 4.M01)

Since an envelope is a small object, the centimeter would be the correct unit of measure.

Answer choices A and C are incorrect because they are used to measure larger objects. Answer choice D is incorrect because it is used to measure long distances.

20. **D** (Number Sense and Operations: 3.N15)

Since all the fractions have 1 as the numerator, look at the denominators. The smaller the denominator the larger the fraction. 1/2 > 1/3 > 1/4. Answer choice D is correct.

Answer choices A, B, and C do not list the fractions from greatest to least.

21. **A** (Algebra: 4.A02)

Answer choice A is correct because:

the number of apples (6) < the number of oranges (7)

the number of apples (6) > the number of bananas (5)

Answer choice B is incorrect because:

the number of apples (5) is not greater than the number of bananas (6)

Answer choice C is incorrect because:

the number of apples (7) is not less than the number of oranges (5)

Answer choice D is incorrect because:

the number of apples (6) is not greater than the number of bananas (7)

22. **C** (Geometry: 3.G02)

Figures that are congruent are the exact same shape and size. The right triangles in answer choice C are congruent figures.

The other answer choices are incorrect because each pair of figures are different sizes.

23. **B** (Number Sense and Operations: 3.N14)

The fraction 6/12 is equal to $\frac{1}{2}$. Answer choice B is correct.

Answer choices A, C, and D are incorrect equivalents for the fraction 6/12.

24. D (Measurement: 4.M09)

From 7:30 A.M. to 8:00 A.M. is 30 minutes. From 8 A.M. to 11 A.M. is 3 hours. The total time is 3 hours 30 minutes. Answer choice D is correct.

Answer choices A, B, and C are wrong due to miscalculation of the time elapsed.

25. B (Number Sense and Operations: 4.N22)

The number sentence for this situation is:

$24 - (9 \times 2)$
$= 24 - 18$
$= 6$

The remainder after 18 hot dogs are eaten is 6. Answer choice B is correct.

Answer choices A, C, and D are incorrect due to miscalculation of the remainder.

26. C (Number Sense and Operations: 4.N15)

The number sentence for how many pull-ups Roberto did is:

$5 + (3 \times 9)$

Viola did 9 pull-ups. Janet did 3 times as many as Viola, which is 3×9 or 27. Roberto did 5 more pull-ups than Janet, or $27 + 5$. Roberto did 32 pull-ups. Answer choice C is correct.

Answer choice A is incorrect because it is the number of pull-ups that Janet did. Answer choices B and D are incorrect due to miscalculation.

27. A (Statistics and Probability: 4.S05)

First, find out how much each student saves each month.

Tamara: 6; Bashir 3; Emily 5, Brett 4.

Next, find the numbers for Month 1. Subtract the number of dollars saved from each person's total for Month 2.

Tamara: 62 – 6 = 56
Bashir: 69 – 3 = 66
Emily: 64 – 5 = 59
Brett: 67 – 4 = 63

Compare the numbers. Tamara had the least number of dollars: 56. Answer choice A is correct.

28. B (Number Sense and Operations: 3.N14)

The diagram of the parking lot is divided into 9 parts. 3 of the parts are shaded to represent an area reserved for buses. The fraction three-ninths = $\frac{1}{3}$. Answer choice B is correct.

Answer choices A, C, and D are incorrect fractions to show the relationship of the shaded area to the entire parking lot.

29. A (Algebra: 4.A01)

If the CIRCLE is greater than the TRIANGLE, and the TRIANGLE is greater than the STAR, then the CIRCLE must also be greater than the STAR. Answer choice A is correct.

Answer choice B is incorrect because the CIRCLE is greater than the STAR.

Answer choice C is incorrect because the STAR is less than the CIRCLE.

Answer choice D is incorrect because the TRIANGLE is greater than the STAR.

30. D (Geometry: 4.G02)

A pentagon is a plane figure with 5 sides. Jackie must draw 3 more line segments to complete the pentagon. Answer choice D is correct.

Answer choices A, B, and C are incorrect because they would result in the wrong number of line segments for the pentagon.

31. 1,453 people (Number Sense and Operations: 4.N14)

32. 581 footballs (Number Sense and Operations: 4.N18)

33. 57 inches (Measurement: 4.M03)

34. Hot Dog, Peanuts, and Fudge Bar (Measurement: 4.M08)

Add the cost of the three items together:

Hot Dog ($2.25) + Peanuts ($1.45) + Fudge Bar ($0.90) = $4.60.

Then subtract the total from $5.00:

$5.00 − $4.60 = $0.40.

J.D. would have $0.40 left over.

35. Part A: 20 units (Geometry: 4.G03)

Remember: 1 unit is 1 face of a square unit.

Part B: 24 square units (Geometry: 4.G04)

36. 5 words (Number Sense and Operations: 4.N22)

$6 \times 9 = 54$

$59 - 54 = 5$

37. 7 teams (Number Sense and Operations: 4.N17)

$7 \times 5 = 35$

38. Part A: $36 (Algebra: 4.A04)

Part B: For every dollar that Maria saves, she gets $4 from her mother.

Every number in Mother's column is 4 times more than the corresponding number in Maria's column.

39. Part A: (Statistics and Probability: 4.S03)

Derek: 11

Alisha: 18

Kaye: 14

Part B:

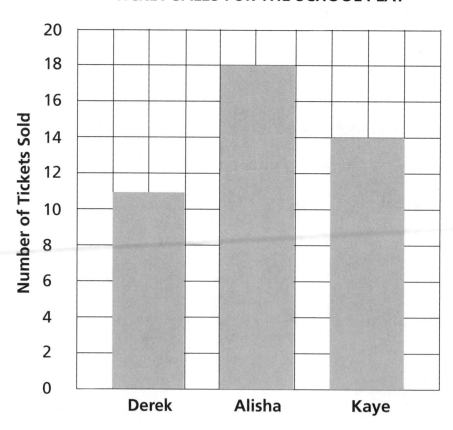

TICKET SALES FOR THE SCHOOL PLAY

40. 104 strawberries (Number Sense and Operations: 4.N18)

41. 34 feet (Geometry: 4.G03)

9 + 8 + 2 + 4 + 7 + 4 = 34

42. $6.05 (Measurement: 4.M08)

43. Part A: (Algebra: 4.A05)

30 necklaces

Each week Suong adds 5 more necklaces to the total number. On Week 5, she had made 25. So on Week 6 she would have 25 + 5 or 30 necklaces.

Part B: Week 9

44. Part A: (Number Sense and Operations: 3.N20)

108 eggs

Part B: 5 × 12 = 60

45. 81 (Algebra: 4.A04)

Rule: Each number in the pattern is 3 times the number before it.

46. 19 marbles (Number Sense and Operations: 4.N21)

57 ÷ 3 = 19

47. (Statistics and Probability: 4.S03)

LOW TEMPERATURES IN BUFFALO, N.Y.

Day	Temperature (° F)
Sunday	8
Monday	13
Tuesday	6
Wednesday	10

48. Part A: Number Sense and Operations: 4.N06)

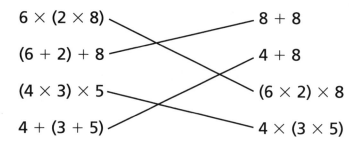

$6 \times (2 \times 8)$ $8 + 8$

$(6 + 2) + 8$ $4 + 8$

$(4 \times 3) \times 5$ $(6 \times 2) \times 8$

$4 + (3 + 5)$ $4 \times (3 \times 5)$

Part B: $5 \times (2 \times 4)$

Practice Test 2 Answer Explanations

1.   **A**   (Number Sense and Operations: 4.N02)

"Nine thousand seven hundred thirty-eight" is the same as the number 9,738. Answer choice A is correct.

Answer choice B is incorrect because it is "nine thousand three hundred seventy-eight." Answer choice C is incorrect because it is "nine thousand thirty-eight." Answer choice D is incorrect because it is "nine hundred thirty-eight."

2.   **C**   (Measurement: 4.M02)

Measure the pencil with the centimeters part of your ruler. The pencil is exactly 13 centimeters long.

Answer choices A, B, and D are incorrect because they are the wrong measurements for the pencil.

3. **B** (Number Sense and Operations: 4.N26)

    To round 932 to the nearest hundred, look at the digit in the tens place. This digit is 3, which is less than 5. Round down to the nearest hundred. The correct answer is 900.

    Answer choice A is incorrect because it was rounded down to 800, not 900. Answer choice C is incorrect because it was rounded to the nearest ten. Answer choice D is incorrect because it was rounded up to 1,000 instead of down to 900.

4. **B** (Number Sense and Operations: 4.N20)

    800 is a multiple of 100. 800 divided by 100 = 8. It takes 8 days for Lena to shoot 800 free throws. Answer choice B is correct.

    Answer choices A, C, and D are all incorrect due to faulty division.

5. **D** (Geometry: 4. G04)

    The sheet of paper is divided into 6 rows, with 11 squares in each row. To get the area, multiply 6 x 11, which is 66. Answer choice D is correct.

    Answer choices A, B, and C are incorrect because of miscounting the squares or faulty multiplication.

6. **A** (Number Sense and Operations: 4.N02)

    The correct words for the number 7,299 are "seven thousand two hundred ninety-nine." Answer choice A is correct.

    Answer choice B is the same as 7,290. Answer choice C is the same as 7,029. Answer choice D is the same as 799.

7. **C** (Number Sense and Operations: 4.N13)

    An odd number multiplied by any odd number always results in an odd number. The only odd number among the answers is 5. Answer choice C is correct.

    Answer choices A, B, and D are all incorrect because they are even numbers.

8. **C** (Number Sense and Operations: 3.N19)

Nine packages of 8 buns is 9 x 8 or 72. Answer choice C is correct.

Answer choices A, B, and D are incorrect products of 9 and 8.

9. **D** (Number Sense and Operations: 3.N20)

12 tables with 7 chairs at each table:
= 12×7
= $(10 + 2) \times 7$
= $(10 \times 7) + (2 \times 7)$
= $70 + 14$
= 84
Answer choice D is correct.

Answer choices A, B, and C are all incorrect due to multiplication problems.

10. **B** (Geometry: 4.G01)

A polygon with eight sides and eight angles is called an octagon. (The prefix *octa*- means "eight.") Answer choice B is correct.

Answer choices A, C, and D are incorrect because they name polygons with the wrong number of sides and angles.

11. **A** (Number Sense and Operations: 4.N17)

Use the inverse operation, or opposite operation, to check an answer. The inverse operation of multiplication is division. $3 \times 12 = 36$, so the number sentence is solved correctly. Answer choice A is correct.

Answer choice B is incorrect because it does not use the inverse operation. Answer choices C and D are incorrect because the wrong two numbers are multiplied together.

12. B (Statistics and Probability: 4.S06)

Check each statement by reading the numbers in the graph. There are 6 cars in the parking lot, and 3 trucks. Six is exactly two times 3. Answer choice B is correct.

Answer choice A is incorrect because there are 13 total vehicles and 6 is not one-half of 13. Answer choice C is incorrect because there are 4 buses and 2 x 4 is not 6. Answer choice D is incorrect because there are 6 cars and 6 is not one-half of 13.

13. D (Number Sense and Operations: 4.N04)

The difference between the two scores is 10,000. In the place value structure of the base ten number system, 10,000 = ten thousands. Answer choice D is correct.

Answer choice A is incorrect because it equals 100. Answer choice B is incorrect because it equals 1,000. Answer choice C is incorrect because it equals 5,000.

14. D (Algebra: 3.A01)

The symbol $>$ means "greater than." The correct answer must be greater than 125. Of the four choices, only 126 is greater than 125. Answer choice D is correct.

Answer choices A and B are incorrect because they are less than 125. Answer choice C is incorrect because it is equal to 125.

15. C (Number Sense and Operations: 4.N06)

Use the Associative Property of Multiplication: $a \times (b \times c) = (a \times b) \times c$. Answer choice C is correct.

Answer choice A is incorrect because the three numbers are added together, not multiplied. Answer choice B is incorrect because 36 is added to (21 x 53), not multiplied. Answer choice D is incorrect because 53 and 36 are added together, not multiplied.

16. C   (Measurement: 4.M04)

The most appropriate unit of measurement listed is the meter.

Answer choice A is incorrect because a centimeter is too small a unit. Answer choice B is incorrect because an inch is also too small a unit. Answer choice D is incorrect because a kilometer is much too large a unit.

17. D   (Algebra: 4.A05)

Answer choice D is correct.

$$1 \times 2 = 2$$
$$3 \times 2 = 6$$
$$5 \times 2 = 10$$
$$7 \times 2 = 14$$

Answer choice A is incorrect because the rule for it is input ÷ 2 = output. Answer choice B is incorrect because the rule for it is input × 3 = output. Answer choice C is incorrect because the rule for it is input + 2 = output.

18. B   (Number Sense and Operations: 4.N27)

To estimate, round 42 down to 40 and round 392 up to 400. 400 divided by 40 = 10. Answer choice B is correct.

Answer choice A is incorrect because it rounds 42 down to 30. Answer choice C is incorrect because it rounds 42 down to 30 and 392 down to 300. Answer choice D is incorrect because it rounds 392 down to 300.

19. A   (Measurement: 4.M01)

The correct unit of measurement for a small amount of sugar is the gram.

Answer choice B is incorrect because the kilogram would be used for larger amounts. Answer choices C and D are incorrect because these units would be used for liquids.

20. A (Number Sense and Operations: 3.N15)

All the fractions have the same numerator: 1. The smallest fraction is the one with the largest denominator: $\frac{1}{4}$. The next smallest is $\frac{1}{3}$, and then $\frac{1}{2}$. Answer choice A is correct.

Answer choices B, C, and D do not list the fractions from greatest to least.

21. B (Algebra: 4.A02)

Answer choice B is correct because:

the number of hamsters (5) > the number of dogs (4)

the number of cats (3) < the number of dogs (4)

Answer choice A is incorrect because:

the number of hamsters (4) is not greater than the number of dogs (5)

Answer choice C is incorrect because:

the number of cats (4) is not less than the number of dogs (3)

Answer choice D is incorrect because:

the number of hamsters (3) is not greater than the number of dogs (4)

22. D (Geometry: 3.G02)

Figures that are similar are the same shape but not necessarily the same size. The triangles in answer choice D are similar figures.

The other answer choices are incorrect because the figures in each pair are not the same shape.

23. A (Number Sense and Operations: 3.N14)

For the fraction 2/6, both the numerator and denominator can be divided by 2. This gives you the fraction $\frac{1}{3}$. Answer choice A is correct.

Answer choices B, C, and D are not equivalent fractions to 2/6.

24. C   (Measurement: 4.M09)

The period from 1:30 P.M. to 4:00 P.M. is 2 hours 30 minutes. Answer choice C is correct.

Answer choices A, B, and D are incorrect due to faulty calculation of time.

25. B   (Number Sense and Operations: 4.N22)

The number sentence for this situation is:

$22 - (5 \times 3)$

$= 22 - 15$

$= 7$

Answer choices A, C, and D are incorrect remainders for this problem.

26. A   (Number Sense and Operations: 4.N15)

Claire can do 3 times as many sit-ups as Tim, and Tim can do 5 more than 15. The number sentence for this problem is:

$3 \times (5 + 15)$

$= 3 \times 20$

$= 60$

Answer choice A is correct.

Answer choices B, C, and D are incorrect due to faulty calculations.

27. B   (Statistics and Probability: 4.S05)

Henry saves 5 dollars each month. His total for month 5 would be 45 (the total at month 3) + 5 + 5 or 55 dollars.

Olivia saves 6 dollars each month. Her total for month 5 would be 45 + 6 + 6 or 57 dollars.

Mina saves 4 dollars each month. Her total for month 5 would be 44 + 4 + 4 or 52 dollars.

Tony saves 3 dollars each month. His total for month 5 would be 44 + 3 + 3 or 50 dollars.

Olivia has the most dollars at the end of month 5. Answer choice B is correct.

28. D (Number Sense and Operations: 3.N14)

The diagram of the park is divided into 8 parts. 2 of the parts are shaded to represent sand. The fraction $\frac{2}{8} = \frac{1}{4}$. Answer choice D is correct.

Answer choices A, B, and C are incorrect fractions to show the relationship of the shaded area to the whole park.

29. C (Algebra: 4.A01)

If the STAR is less than the CIRCLE, and the CIRCLE is less than the TRIANGLE, then the STAR must be less than the TRIANGLE. In other words, the TRIANGLE is greater than the STAR. Answer choice C is correct.

Answer choice A is incorrect because the CIRCLE is less than the TRIANGLE.

Answer choice B is incorrect because the STAR is less than the CIRCLE.

Answer choice D is incorrect because the STAR is less than the TRIANGLE.

30. B (Geometry: 4.G02)

A hexagon is a plane figure with 6 sides. Mark must draw 4 more line segments to complete the hexagon. Answer choice B is correct.

Answer choices A, C, and D are incorrect because they would result in the wrong number of line segments for the hexagon.

31. 1,024 people (Number Sense and Operations: 4.N14)

32. 456 trucks (Number Sense and Operations: 4.N18)

33. 68 inches (Measurement: 4.M03)

34. Hot Dog, Cheese Nachos, and Lemonade (Measurement: 4.M08)

Add the cost of the three items together:

Hot Dog ($3.25) + Cheese Nachos ($3.50) + Lemonade ($2.50) = $9.25.

Then subtract the total from $10.00:

$10.00 − $9.25 = $0.75.

Jolene would have $0.75 left.

35. Part A: 30 units (Geometry: 4.G03)

Remember: 1 unit is 1 face of a square unit.

Part B: 54 square units (Geometry: 4.G04)

36. 2 names (Number Sense and Operations: 4.N22)

$6 \times 7 = 42$

$44 − 42 = 2$

37. 8 flowers (Number Sense and Operations: 4.N17)

$7 \times 8 = 56$

38. Part A: $30 (Algebra: 4.A04)

Part B: For every dollar that Walter saves, he gets $3 from his dad.

Every number in Dad's column is 3 times more than the corresponding number in Walter's column.

39. Part A: (Statistics and Probability: 4.S03)

Lucinda: 14
Alex: 16
Marta: 19

Part B:

BOOKS READ IN THE CONTEST

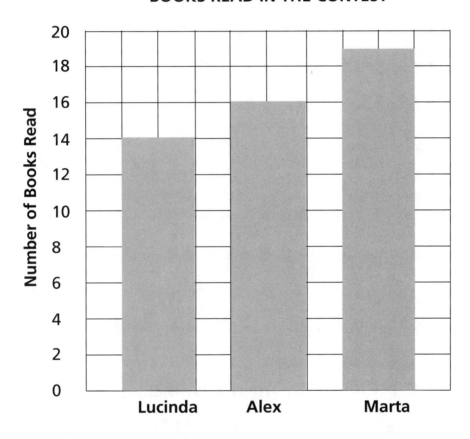

40. 12 puppets (Number Sense and Operations: 4.N18)

72 ÷ 6 = 12

41. 24 yards (Geometry: 4.G03)

3 + 5 + 2 + 2 + 5 + 7 = 24

42. $0.79 (Measurement: 4.M08)

43. **Part A:** (Algebra: 4.A05)

    56 belt buckles

    Each week Mr. Sanchez adds 7 more belt buckles to the total number. On Week 6, he had made 42. So on Week 8 he would have 42 + 7 + 7 or 56 belt buckles.

    Part B: Week 11

44. **Part A:** (Number Sense and Operations: 3.N20)

    77 pens

    Part B: $4 \times 7 = 28$

45. 33 (Algebra: 4.A04)

    Rule: Each number in the pattern is 3 less than the number before it.

46. 90 blue beads (Number Sense and Operations: 4.N21)

    $15 \times 6 = 90$

47. (Statistics and Probability: 4.S03)

HOME RUNS HIT BY THE N.Y. YANKEES

Month of the Season	Number of Home Runs
May	25
June	20
July	10
August	35